Power Time Management

More Time, Less Stress,
and Zero Procrastination
(Your Breakthrough for More Success,
Happiness and Time Off)

Tom Marcoux

America's Communication Coach
TFG Thought Leader
Speaker-Author of 24 books
Blogger, BeHeardandBeTrusted.com

A QuickBreakthrough Publishing Edition

Copyright © 2014 Tom Marcoux Media, LLC
ISBN: 0692235256
ISBN-13: 978-0692235256

All rights reserved. No part of this book may be reproduced or transmitted in any form by any means electronic or mechanical, including photocopying, recording or by any information storage and retrieval system without written permission from the publisher.

QuickBreakthrough Publishing is an imprint of Tom Marcoux Media, LLC. More copies are available from the publisher, Tom Marcoux Media, LLC. Please call (415) 572-6609 or write TomSuperCoach@gmail.com

or visit www.TomSuperCoach.com

or Tom's blog: www.BeHeardandBeTrusted.com

This book was developed and written with care. Names and details were modified to respect privacy.

Disclaimer: The author and publisher acknowledge that each person's situation is unique, and that readers have full responsibility to seek consultations with health, financial, spiritual and legal professionals. The author and publisher make no representations or warranties of any kind, and the author and publisher shall not be liable for any special, consequential or exemplary damages resulting, in whole or in part, from the reader's use of, or reliance upon, this material.:

Other Books by Tom Marcoux:
- Be Heard and Be Trusted: How to Get What You Want
- Nothing Can Stop You This Year!
- Reduce Clutter, Enlarge Your Life
- Darkest Secrets of Persuasion and Seduction Masters
- Darkest Secrets of Charisma
- Darkest Secrets of Negotiation Masters
- Darkest Secrets of the Film and Television Industry Every Actor Should Know
- Darkest Secrets of Making a Pitch to the Film and Television Industry
- Darkest Secrets of Film Directing
- Truth No One Will Tell You

Praise for *Power Time Management* and Tom Marcoux
• "In *Power Time Management*, Tom Marcoux shares his extraordinary strategies and methods that save you time, make you money and increase your success and happiness. As Tom's client for many years, I have benefited from his wisdom and strategic approach. Do your career and personal life a big favor and get this book!" – Dr. JoAnn Dahlkoetter, author of *Your Performing Edge* and coach to CEOs and Olympic Gold Medalists
• "You'll be inspired by Tom Marcoux's sincere efforts to help you resolve problems. I recommend his work to anyone in a pickle."
– David Barron, co-author of *Power Persuasion*

Praise for Tom Marcoux's Other Work:
• "In *Reduce Clutter, Enlarge Your Life*, Marcoux will help you get rid of the physical and mental clutter occupying precious space in your life. You'll reclaim wasted energy, lower your stress, and find time for new opportunities." – Laura Stack, author of *Execution IS the Strategy*
• "*Create Your Best Life* helps you learn skills in persuasion, charisma, confidence, influence and emotional strength. To make a dream come true, you'll need to get people enrolled in your vision. This is *the book* that helps you get great things done!" – Dr. JoAnn Dahlkoetter, author of *Your Performing Edge* and coach to CEOs and Olympic Gold Medalists
• "In *Darkest Secrets of Persuasion and Seduction Masters*, learn useful countermeasures to protect you from being darkly manipulated."
– David Barron, co-author, *Power Persuasion*
• "In *Be Heard and Be Trusted*, Tom's advice on how to remain true to yourself and establish authentic rapport with clients is both insightful and reality based. He [shows how] to establish oneself as a credible expert."
-Arthur P. Ciaramicoli, Ed.D., Ph.D., author *The Curse of the Capable*
• "*Nothing Can Stop You This Year* is a treasure trove of tips, tools, and terrific ideas—practical, reassuring, and energizing! Tom provides wonderful resources for achieving your goals." – Elayne Savage, Ph.D., author of *Don't Take It Personally! The Art of Dealing with Rejection*

Visit Tom's blog: www.BeHeardandBeTrusted.com

Tom Marcoux

CONTENTS

Dedication and Acknowledgments	I
Book One: Your Power to Get Yourself to Take Action	7

Articles are interspersed in this book . . . by guest authors Mark Sanborn, Mike Robbins, Patricia Fripp, Randy Gage, Steve Rizzo, Jeanna Gabellini, Chip Conley, Rebecca Morgan, Cheryl Wood, Dr. Elayne Savage, Jean Moroney and Ed Gandia.

Book Two: Your Power to Leap Forward and Increase Success	49
Book Three: Your Power to Make More Money	87
Book Four: Your Power to Save Time and Get the Best from People	125
Book Five: Your Power to Take More Time Off	143
Book Six: Your Power to Increase Happiness and Enhance Loving Relationships	171
A Final Word and Springboard to Your Success	205
Excerpt from *Darkest Secrets of Persuasion and Seduction Masters: How to Protect Yourself and Turn the Power to Good*	207
About the Author Tom Marcoux	214
Special Offer Just for Readers of this Book	216

DEDICATION AND ACKNOWLEDGEMENTS

This book is dedicated to the terrific book and film consultant, and author Johanna E. Mac Leod. It is also dedicated to the other team members. Thanks to Sherry Lusk and David MacDowell Blue for editing.

Thanks to guest authors Mark Sanborn, Mike Robbins, Patricia Fripp, Randy Gage, Steve Rizzo, Jeanna Gabellini, Chip Conley, Rebecca Morgan, Cheryl Wood, Dr. Elayne Savage, Jean Moroney and Ed Gandia. [Their articles remain with their original copyright and are included in this book by their permission.]

Thanks to Judita Bacinskaite for rendering this book's front cover. Thank you Johanna E. Mac Leod for the back cover. Thanks to my father, Al Marcoux, for his concern and efforts for me. Thanks to my mother, Sumiyo Marcoux, a kind, generous soul. Thank you to Higher Power. Thanks to our readers, audiences, clients, my graduate/college students and my team members of
Tom Marcoux Media, LLC. The best to you.

BOOK ONE:
YOUR POWER TO GET YOURSELF TO TAKE ACTION

I lay dying and I had one thought on my mind. My father looked at the wound on my chest, and he couldn't do a thing to help me. I was bleeding out.

"There's so much left to do," I kept thinking.

And then in tears, I woke up.

Several years ago, that was my horrible nightmare.

That's when I began **a quest for Power Time Management.** There was so much I deeply wanted to do.

What do YOU truly want to do?

Is procrastination slowing you down?

Have you become really frustrated with your own time management practices?

Does success feel out of reach?

Standard time management leaves so many of us frustrated and stuck. Why? Because some speakers and authors attempt to foist a paint-by-number system upon us. Perhaps, you know people who hate their day planners and don't use them well. There are many who write To-Do Lists, and they end up "I Didn't" Lists.

However, here's the truth that I've learned in 25 years of coaching people: **You need to listen to your own style, your own heart and your own needs.** A coach can help you with that and help you uncover what will most benefit your life *now*. Through this book, I serve as your coach.

Power Time Management is so much better than standard list making. Have you noticed that a To-Do List really acts like a Guilt List? We tend to feel guilty about the tasks we fail to complete on a given day.

What we need is *something better* than standard time management...

The Real Benefits of Power Time Management:
- save time
- get more done in less time
- reduce stress and worry
- increase success faster
- change behavior to achieve what you really want
- find time to experience relaxation, joy, and time with loved ones
- Increase your personal happiness

I began this book, sharing my experience of a terrible dream, because I've always remembered the sheer power of the emotions I felt.

These emotions pushed me to study, get coaching with mentors, and earn a degree in psychology. Employing my skills, I taught over 5,241 graduate students and college students.

I've coached hundreds people from MBA students at Stanford University to workshop attendees at Sun Microsystems, Silicon Valley Bank and IBM.

How did I help them increase their productivity? I impart

the methods I used to get so much done: I've written 24 books, directed feature films, composed music and more.

One of my skills is to boil down a lot of research data and strategies into bite-sized, *memorable* patterns.

The essence of *Power Time Management* is E.A.R. – remember I mentioned *listen to yourself*?

E - energy
A - action
R – replace procrastination

Power Time Management also involves something unusual; it helps you increase skills for building relationships based on trust.

One of my innovations focuses on *The Charisma Advantage that Saves Time*. I explain this as: "When I help you enhance charisma, people trust you faster. Trust saves time."

We'll explore the material in these sections noted as Books One through Six:

- Your Power to Get Yourself to Take Action
- Your Power to Leap Forward and Increase Success
- Your Power to Make More Money
- Your Power to Save Time and Get the Best from People
- Your Power to Take More Time Off
- Your Power to Increase Happiness and Enhance Loving Relationships

Let's begin . . .

BOOK ONE CONTINUES: YOUR POWER TO GET YOURSELF TO TAKE ACTION

Power Time Management makes you more powerful than standard list-making in conventional time management. **Power Time Management empowers you to take action.**

In this section we'll cover these topics:

- How You Can Change Your Mood and Get More Done
- Overcome 3 Big Mistakes of Standard Time Management
- How You Can Get More Done and Feel Better Doing It
- Power to Overcome Procrastination
- Handle Risk Well and Leap Forward to Success
- Use a Simple, Powerful Method for Amazing Results

HOW YOU CAN CHANGE YOUR MOOD AND GET MORE DONE
(#1 of Get Yourself to Take Action)

Can you imagine how much more you'd get done if you weren't slowed down by a bad mood? To improve your productivity, it helps to have a plan so that you can change your mood in many instances. Sure, you may not be able to change a bad mood every time, but I learned something valuable from one of my mentors, the late Richard Carlson, author of *Don't Sweat the Small Stuff*. He told me, "It's not that I never get stressed out. It's that I *spend much less time* stressed out than before."

Some time ago, I had a team member who was responsible for the technology in my office. It was his job to make sure all intellectual property was backed up in multiple places. Unfortunately, "Matthew" made an error and a significant number of book covers and other items were not backed up.

Fortunately, I was not frantic about my writing projects because I personally back up files daily. However, a number of book covers were *gone!* One of our book cover designers (a contractor) proved unreachable. So one of our *new* book covers went out with a *bad small image* on the back cover.

Ooh! I'm feeling upset about this again!

Now, letting myself go into a bad mood would not help me, Matthew or my team.

So I fall back on the idea "I *spend less time* stressed out than before."

I immediately ask myself these questions:
- What can I do now to make this better?
- What do I control in this situation?

- How can I guide Matthew to do better from this moment forward?

Another powerful way to change my mood is to focus on this idea:

Life is about success, <u>not</u> perfection. – Alan Weiss

This reminds me that an error on a cover can be fixed. As a human being I can prioritize what needs the highest levels of excellence—and what can be "good enough."

I'll now share the following F.E.E.L. process. (The idea is to *feel better*.)

F – focus on what you can control
E – enter your Low Mood First Aid Kit
E – encourage yourself to "face it, feel it, let go"
L – linger for 10 positive seconds

1. Focus on what you can control

Have you noticed that the more you focus on things you cannot control, the worse you feel?

Let's face it: you cannot control another person's feelings, preferences or behaviors.

Sometimes you may have a bit of influence. But often, we do not have such influence.

So what do you control? Your own behavior.

Actions seems to follow feeling, but really actions and feeling go together; and by regulating the action, which is under the more direct control of the will, we can indirectly regulate the feeling, which is not. – William James

Author Stephen R. Covey wrote about what we can and cannot control. He made a good point that we have two different "circles": a Circle of Concern and a Circle of Influence.

Think of it this way: If your Circle of Concern matches your Circle of Influence, you're happy. On the other hand, if you're focused on things that you cannot control, you're likely upset. That's when you're focused on things *outside the intersection* of your Circle of Concern and Circle of Influence.

Become proactive. Consciously choose to focus on your Circle of Influence—that is, focus on what you *can* control in a situation. And, as mentioned, that is likely your *own* behavior.

2. Enter your *Low Mood First Aid Kit*

By *enter your Low Mood First Aid Kit*, I mean consult your list of possible activities that can uplift your mood.

My clients have mentioned their actions:
- listen to a relaxing piece of music
- take a brief walk
- call a positive friend
- look at photos of happy times with family
- relax in a warm, soothing bath

It's helpful to have a list of things you can do that do NOT require the presence or cooperation of another person. For example, I truly enjoy making progress. I can do that simply by pulling out my tablet computer and writing a paragraph.

Another reason I used the verb "enter" is that when you do a relaxing or uplifting activity, you can temporarily enter a "relaxing world." For example, when I listen to uplifting music, I'm transported to another state of being.

Now, I invite you to make a list for *your* Low Mood First

Aid Kit. Carry this list with you so that you can reach for it in times of discomfort.

3. Encourage yourself to "face it, feel it, let go"

Have you noticed that sometimes it takes feeling something deeply, crying and then you can finally move on?

I've experienced that a few times with the ending of a romantic relationship.

On a couple of occasions, seeing a film helped me have an emotional release. At the end of a relationship, I cried during the part of *Superman II* when Superman had to give up his love with Lois Lane so that he could continue to be the on-call guardian of the world.

Some years later, I was feeling terrible at the end of a romantic relationship, then I saw *Pocahontas* (the Disney film) and cried during the filmed sequence to the song "Colors of the Wind."

I invite you to consider giving yourself the space to feel what you need to feel so that you can move forward.

4. Linger for 10 positive seconds

In my book *10 Seconds to Wealth*, I discussed the research that notes that it takes 10 to 20 seconds of focused attention to place a positive experience into your long term memory.

To be able to change into a positive mood, it helps for you to "practice positive feelings." By this I mean, you need to store positive neural patterns—these are patterns in your brain. The field of neurology has uncovered this fact: "Neurons that fire together tend to wire together." This phrase means that brain cells (neurons) are activated in patterns which often become locked.

Be sure that you have many positive neural patterns that are locked in.

You do that by focusing on the positive. For example, every night in the minutes just before I go to sleep I write down notes about positive experiences of the day. I write these details in my *Daily Journal of Victories and Blessings*. A victory is something that I accomplish like daily exercise. A blessing is something positive that arises—for example, a surprise phone call from a friend.

In people, when a painful or negative situation occurs it instantly goes into long term memory. One reason for this is that our ancestors were those who remembered pain and danger—and they survived! So by heredity, we are the result of all the survivors who stored memories of pain and how to avoid even more pain.

That's why we must take personal control and literally *accentuate the positive—for 10 seconds!*

* * *

To develop the ability to change your mood for the better in many instances requires one thing: effective practice. Focus on:

F – focus on what you can control
E – enter your Low Mood First Aid Kit
E – encourage yourself to "face it, feel it, let go"
L – linger for 10 positive seconds

When you use the F.E.E.L. process, you can truly spend less time in a bad mood. This opens many opportunities for you do more and to feel better while doing it.

Principle

A prime way to feel better is to focus on what you *can* control.

Power Questions

What can you control? How can you change your behaviors so that you start feeling better? What's part of your personal Low Mood First Aid Kit? How can you schedule time to do something that lifts your spirits?

* * * * * *

OVERCOME 3 BIG MISTAKES OF STANDARD TIME MANAGEMENT
(#4 of Get Yourself to Take Action)

Several clients and audience members have told me that they need to improve their time management.

I observe they want to get more done, overcome procrastination and rise to higher levels of success and happiness.

Much of their difficulties reside in **3 Big Mistakes of Standard Time Management:**

1) Letting a long list beat you up emotionally
2) Adding too much to your list and not identifying "Droppables"
3) Allowing your energy to be scattered; letting yourself be pushed around

Now, I'll go through the 3 Big Mistakes and provide solutions:

1) Letting a long list beat you up emotionally
A To-Do List is a collection tool. It does NOT help raise

your energy level or your morale.

In fact, a long To-Do List is often demoralizing.

Here's the solution: *Top Six Targets.*

By *Top Six Targets* I mean that you write a list at the end of your workday or just before you go to sleep that includes the most important items. These items would help you feel like you had a productive and focused day.

With my audiences, I suggest: "2 for work, 2 for you, 2 for family."

The point is to identify the six things you can do so that you have a good day, a successful day.

It is most likely that you cannot complete all the tasks on the 25 item list. But you *can* get your Top Six Targets done. And you'll feel good and energized about it.

2) Adding too much to your list and not identifying "Droppables"

When I first used a Day Planner, I discovered two things: a) I overscheduled my time and b) I found my To-Do List to be a Guilt List. That is, I felt bad every night as I carried over to the next day all the things I did not complete. Now, I suggest that you again consider the value of *Top Six Targets*. I write my Top Six Target on a 3 x 5 card each night.

Further, in addition to priorities, you need "Droppables" which are those tasks that you strategically drop from your schedule. **So that's a solution for this section: Select your Droppables.**

Later in this book, I share strategies for effective delegation. Meanwhile, you need to make good choices.

For example, in my book *Reduce Clutter, Enlarge Your Life*, I shared the example of a Droppable. When I was getting rid of 243 boxes of stuff and keeping only those things I treasured, I made an important decision about a Droppable.

Anyone who has sorted and let go of a lot of stuff knows that the process is quite physical and exhausting. So my Droppable was to skip my usual use of a treadmill and weights. Why? I just didn't have the energy to spare. I used my moving of banker boxes as my exercise regimen for the 17 days in which I removed the 243 boxes from my life.

Be sure to identify Droppables. You may not have the time or energy to do "everything"—but you *can* make good choices and do that which is *most important*.

3) Allowing your energy to be scattered; letting yourself be pushed around

Power Time Management is concerned with your personal energy.

The problem with standard time management is that you're just using lists and everyone around you (supervisor, co-workers, customers, family, friends) all want a piece of your time and to get on your calendar.

The truth is: you don't have enough energy for everyone else's priorities AND your own. You need to build up your personal energy and *focus* on your personal priorities.

An important *solution* is to **put yourself on your own calendar. Schedule appointments with yourself.** Such appointments are related to your personal energy.

When I teach audiences about personal energy, I focus on two things (which will function as **the solutions** of this section): a) The Three Sources of Energy and b) the *Positive-Trigger-Pattern*.

a) *The Three Sources of Energy*

The sources of energy include 1) Stop the pain, 2) "For the team," and 3) "I am excited about..."

- **Stop the pain**

Many of us, if we admit it, only really jump into action when we're afraid that inaction will lead to big trouble and big pain. It's valuable to observe that pattern and *use it*. That works for some of my clients when they need to take action related to taxes paperwork. Use what works. Use the source of energy that is practical for you.

- **"For the team"**

Some people will do much more for a loved one than for themselves. I know that I will work more hours and do things I really don't like to do (like filing papers and clearing clutter) to insure that something good happens for a family member. I can use this loving energy to get myself moving forward fast.

- **"I am excited about..."**

Over the years, in coaching clients, audience members and graduate students, I have observed that "stop the pain" is frequently a more potent source of energy than "I am excited about [xy] happening." Research data shows that people will often do more to stop pain than to gain pleasure. However, some of us (including entrepreneurs that I know) really want to *make something happen*. It's that excitement that fueled Steve Jobs to lead teams to do incredible work. If you find that your energy expands as you focus on what you're excited about—use that pattern!

* * *

b) Use a *Positive-Trigger-Pattern* to Replace Procrastination

Start to pick your priorities and set up a related *Positive-Trigger-Pattern*. By this, I mean to observe some trigger in your environment and attach *what you want to do* to the trigger. This will become clear as I give an example:

I often take a train to San Francisco to teach a college level public speaking class. As soon as my rear end hits the seat, I pull out my tablet computer (with keyboard) and start typing words related to my *Jack AngelSword* graphic novels and text-novel.

Sitting in the seat is the trigger. And my example above is a personal Positive-Trigger-Pattern.

Here's the heart of the matter: "Replace procrastination with strategy."

My strategy is to go into immediate action without pausing to worry about how my writing will be. My first 10 minutes can be agony with not liking my own writing, but then I get into the groove.

Inspiration usually comes during work rather than before it.
– Madeleine L'Engle

Here's another point: **Set a positive trigger-plus-action when you're cool so that you act effectively when the situation is "hot."**

The solution is to avoid needing to make a tough, positive choice when you're feeling tempted to procrastinate. **Instead, use strategy to set up your Positive-Trigger-Pattern in advance.** Then you'll automatically do the right thing (similar to how I automatically write on the train).

What Positive-Trigger-Pattern would help your own

efforts to get things done?

Principle
Set a positive trigger-plus-action when you're cool so that you act effectively when the situation is "hot."

Power Questions
What is something you can do that will really improve your life? How can you tie a good action to a trigger in your environment? In other words, how can you set up a Positive-Trigger-Pattern?

* * * * * *

HOW YOU CAN GET MORE DONE AND FEEL BETTER DOING IT
(#3 of Get Yourself to Take Action)

Want to get more done and faster? I'm with you about that. I've been on a quest that has improved my productivity so that I've written 24 books—all on Amazon.com. Here is the P.O.W.E.R. process:

P – pinpoint
O – open
W – win
E – eliminate (let go)
R – refuse to hesitate

1. Pinpoint
Pinpoint your focus. I once placed my company's projects

on a board: a total of 14 projects. I made decisions on each one (postponing, eliminating, quickly finishing). Making those decisions and actions helped me get 14 down to a remaining 4 top priority projects.

2. Open

Open your mind to new and more productive ways to do things. Listen to audio programs, read articles and books. Talk with advisors and mentors. For example, I'm writing this article on a train to San Francisco where I teach my public speaking class for college students. I needed a new computer unit to do my typing. What to get? I talked to my circle of advisors and I'm now typing on a hybrid—a tablet with a detachable keyboard.

3. Win

I emphasize, with my clients, this phrase: "Make it a game you can win." For example, I'm currently writing a novel. I know that if I type a minimum of 383 words a day, I can finish my first draft in 180 days. So I keep track of my progress. I get positive emotional energy for having a clear target. Here are two of my other phrases that are related:

"Keep Score and Achieve More."

"Don't guess: Measure it for success."

4. Eliminate (let go)

When you want to get more done, you'll do well to reduce the amount of time feeling upset and stressed out. In essence, you eliminate time lost to being upset. Here is my P.A.L. system:

a) P – pause and breathe

Do some belly breathing (breathe in deeply and allow your belly to inflate, hold for a moment, breathe out and let your belly deflate). Taking a few moments for belly breathing helps you calm down and think more clearly.

b) A – align

Align with your principles. For example, with an irascible elderly family member, I do not return negativity for negativity. (That's one of my principles.) I save time because I avoid the escalation of bad feelings.

c) L – let go

I use certain phrases to change the direction of my thoughts:

- *I don't run that show.* [For example, I do not control other people's moods or their priorities.]
- *That was a good run.* [For example, I do not control when things change and some organization changes their schedule and certain opportunities go away. By saying, "That was a good run," my thoughts turn to gratitude for the opportunity that I enjoyed previously.]

5. Refuse to hesitate

Recently, a friend asked, "Would you send me a list of your books that I did some editing for?" I said, "I'll do that in the next five minutes." He said, "You don't have to do it now."

I explained, "If I can, I get things done and keep my to-do list smaller."

So I ended our phone call and pulled together the list and sent it to him.

Also, this morning, I had a dream in which my intuition called on me to release a book on time management. So I did not hesitate. To get started, I wrote this section.

[For more about overcoming procrastination and

increasing your productivity: see my book *Nothing Can Stop You This Year!*]

People speak of time management. I prefer talking about Time Leadership or really, personal leadership.

Use strategies to streamline your approach to tasks.

For example, I suggest to my speech audiences: "The night before, write up your ***Top Six Targets*** for the next day. Two for you, two for work, two for family."

Focus on those six, and get the most important things done.

You'll feel better.

Principle
Focus and get the most important things done.

Power Questions
Will you use Top Six Targets to focus on the most important things to accomplish during your day?

* * * * * *

POWER TO OVERCOME PROCRASTINATION
(#4 of Get Yourself to Take Action)

Would you like to overcome procrastination and get more done? Can you imagine how you'd rise to a higher level of success faster?

This reminds me of the time a college student applied to become an intern for my company. I said, "Tell me about a weakness you have." He said, "I'm lazy."

As you can guess, I did NOT hire him.

But I thought about his comment over the next weeks.

Did he say, "I'm lazy" because he truly was lazy? Or was it because *he was disgusted with himself for procrastinating* on projects?

If he attended one of my presentations on "Power Time Management: More Time, Less Stress and Zero Procrastination," I would have informed him that procrastination is formed in a great part by mere bad habits.

Drop the habit of procrastination; replace it with actions that get you going quickly.

For example, as soon as I had a thought about this section of this book, I immediately opened the file and began typing. No hesitation. In other words, I experienced "zero procrastination."

How do I avoid procrastination? Every day, I practice certain patterns of action that help me "replace procrastination" with empowering actions.

In many cases we're talking about training your "Autopilot Coach." Research shows that successful people do certain effective actions automatically. They are not struggling over decisions; they have already made one decision and it forms an automatic habit.

For example, I mention in another section of this book that *I eat salad for breakfast.* So when I approach the refrigerator in the morning, I have no hesitation. I simply open the refrigerator, grab some spinach and throw it into a bowl. Then I add other items: perhaps, a piece of chicken or a slice of turkey formed as meatloaf.

With that one phrase "I eat salad for breakfast," I have trained my Autopilot Coach to guide my decisions.

Now, it may seem that eating salad for breakfast is not about avoiding procrastination, but I mentioned it above because I literally save time in the morning during my "prime time." My mornings are the best time for my writing so I do *not* want to lose precious minutes of my "prime time."

Now, I'll share the G.O.N.O.W. process.

The G.O.N.O.W. process to Overcome Procrastination:

G – get the pain out
O – offer fun
N – nurture "Self-Rewards"
O – open the "pain-valve"
W – wrangle schedules

1. Get the pain out

Ask any college instructor about the bane of their existence, and they'll mention grading papers. One way I take pain out of the experience is to listen to uplifting music while grading.

What can you do that would get rid of some pain in doing an onerous task? For instance, can you take your laptop computer to the porch and write while enjoying the outdoors?

2. Offer fun

Can you go a step further and add fun to the process? For example, one of my clients, sets up a "paperwork-plus-dinner" evening with a friend. Both friends did taxes-related paperwork for one hour and then they had dinner together. Afterwards, they did an additional hour of paperwork. They worked on their own paperwork but having a loving friend in the room added some fun to the mix.

When I write a first draft section of a book, I have fun by reading it out loud to a team member. While I'm reading it and getting her feedback, I'm also improving the work. I enjoy the comradery we share as the project improves. I really enjoy making progress.

3. Nurture "Self-Rewards"

Sometimes, only the promise of a valued reward can get us moving. One of my clients uses the treadmill in the morning and then purchases a drink at Starbucks® on the way to work. By promising herself the reward of Starbucks®, she motivates herself to complete her physical activity.

Do not wait for anyone else to offer you a reward. Instead, develop your own rewards. This is related to my phrase: *Keep Score and Achieve More*. Identify what you want to accomplish, keep score, and give yourself a "Self-Reward" (a reward you give to yourself).

If you have a report to do work, set up small milestones and deadlines over the three weeks that you have to complete the project. Do not wait to receive accolades at the completion of the project. Give yourself small rewards for meeting a series of due dates (for section one, section two, and so on).

4. Open the "pain-valve"

Many of us only get into action when we fully feel the dread of a bad outcome happening. One of my clients only gets moving on taxes paperwork when she thinks about avoiding tax penalties. I have helped her realize that a tax penalty will "steal from her" the vacation she has been longing for. At that point, she gets angry "about the injustice of it" and takes action and gets her taxes paperwork done.

To "open the pain-valve" means to visualize and fully feel what painful experience will happen if you fail to take action.

Another client wants a healthier relationship with his wife. He visualizes her criticism if he does not replace the toilet roll in their bathroom. Now, he consistently replaces the toilet roll and another irritant is *absent* from their relationship.

What painful outcome do you want to avoid? How would you get hurt if you fail to take action? What can you do now to get moving and get something done toward removing that potential painful situation or even disaster? Get moving.

5. Wrangle schedules

When I say, "wrangle schedules," I'm talking about fitting an onerous task into "natural transition points." Between activities, you may have a few minutes (a transition point), and that can help you get something done.

For example, after a large meal at a restaurant, I announced to family members, "As soon as we get home, I'm getting on the treadmill for 15 minutes." As soon as I arrived in my home, I immediately began exercising on my treadmill. There was no hesitation. This is another example of "zero procrastination."

Further, I called a friend, and we had a pleasant conversation while I was exercising. In having a good time, I easily increased my time on the treadmill from 15 minutes to 31 minutes.

For example, one of my clients, Shirley, was waiting for a friend to arrive for a get-together. That friend was running late so Shirley took those 15 minutes and washed a portion of her bathtub. She was pleased with her progress. It took two more brief sessions, and Shirley completed cleaning her bathtub within two days.

Another client tosses laundry into her washing machine in her garage just before she gets into the car. Then she is joined by her romantic partner in the car. After they return from the grocery store, she hangs up the clothes while her romantic partner carries the food upstairs.

How can you "wrangle your schedule?" That is, how can you place onerous tasks into "natural transition points"?

Principle

To overcome procrastination, it helps to pre-plan how you will take action. Use the G.O.N.O.W. process to set a plan and then take action.

Power Questions

What really pushes you into action? Do you need to visualize a painful outcome and then take action to avoid bad consequences? Or do you need to motivate yourself with schedule of small victories augmented by Self-Rewards?

* * * * * *

HANDLE RISK WELL AND LEAP FORWARD FOR SUCCCESS
(#5 of Get Yourself to Take Action)

Would you like to handle risk well for greater success? Several years ago, risk meant to me that I clung by my fingertips to the hood of a speeding, cherry-red, classic 50s

Chevy truck—a movie stunt. I was director, lead actor and stuntman. Would I do the same stunt today? Unlikely. Still, I've faced many risks: teaching MBA students at Stanford University, speaking in front of 709 people at the National Association of Broadcasters Conference, and more. I've learned powerful methods for dealing well with risk. And these methods form a vital part of my Power Time Management process.

Now, we'll study the R.I.S.K. methods:

R – reduce the downside

I – identify the voice of fear and the voice of intuition

S – set "levels of success"

K – keep learning

1. Reduce the downside

The downside includes anything that can go wrong when you take a risk. And, because there can be big problems, I prefer to take an "appropriate risk." It is not, at this time, an appropriate risk for me to go bouldering—that's when you climb a mountain without ropes holding you to the side of the mountain.

I do not have the appropriate knowledge or body conditioning for such a feat. More importantly, it is *not* important enough for me to prepare for bouldering.

When something is important to me, *I prepare* so that I can reduce the downside.

"Reduce the downside" has a big impact on your Power Time Management: When you know how you'll be able to recover from something going wrong, *you will reduce hesitation* to taking action.

Pay close attention to your "want-power." When you want something enough, you'll do a lot of preparation.

Be clear about the downside and what you'll do to reduce

it. Use questions like these:
- What are the worst things that could happen?
- How can I prepare so that I will not fall apart if the worst things happen?
- How can I study, work with a coach and get appropriate guidance when I'm going into a new area of activity?
- How can I prepare, rehearse and become stronger so that the worst thing is LESS likely to occur?
- What will I do to reduce the damage if things go wrong?
- How will I emerge stronger and smarter by going through this situation?

Make excellent plans that take care of any concerns raised by the above questions.

While working with my clients, I often emphasize: **You reduce risk by rehearsing well.**

2. Identify the voice of fear and the voice of intuition

To handle risk well, it's important to identify two voices in your mind: the voice of fear and the voice of intuition.

Here is a quick comparison:

Voice of fear: contract, hide, don't take a risk

Voice of intuition: expand, experiment, take appropriate risks, explore—Live!

People stuck in the voice of fear become paralyzed. They stay in their comfort zone. Almost by definition, a person who is stuck in fear gets *less* things done.

But this is NOT for you.

Listen to yourself. At the beginning of this book I

mentioned that Power Time Management focuses on E.A.R. – energy, action and replace procrastination.

When you focus on your voice of intuition, you get inspired: Your energy expands!

Finally, when I talk with clients about the voice of intuition, I ask:

"Are you building something?"

That is, are you building some aspect of your life? If you want to be a filmmaker, it's worth making several short films to build up your filmmaking skills.

Realize that taking appropriate risks will likely expand your enjoyment of life.

3. Set "levels of success"

One filmmaker I know, "Frieda," had three goals for her independent feature film:

1) People will see and enjoy the film. (We serve viewers.)
2) The actors and crew will further their careers.
3) We (investors, actors, crew) will make money.

She told me: "We got two out of three. Next time, I'll do better with the make-money part."

The good news is that Frieda and her team did accomplish a good "level of success." They did make a film that showcases their capabilities, and many of the team members have had further opportunities in the film industry due to their involvement in Frieda's film.

When you set "levels of success," you can be both optimistic and realistic. There are times when our fondest hopes do not pan out. But if you plan and take action to get some progress and forward movement, you succeed on some level. I say this phrase often: "Better than zero." Doing nothing gives you "zero." Doing something gives you real-world experience. That can be truly helpful on your journey.

4. Keep learning

Many years ago, George Lucas made *THX-1138* as his first feature film. Much of the film was considered experimental and the film was largely ignored. After that film, George studied with Joseph Campbell, author of *The Hero with a Thousand Faces* and famed proponent of the "hero's journey." Campbell had observed that cultures around the world had similarities in storytelling.

George learned these storytelling elements from Campbell, and then George infused *Star Wars* with them. Yes!—*Star Wars* did appeal to millions of people throughout the world and to generations of fans.

That's the power of learning. You can create something that has a significant impact. Researchers have discovered that top performers in various disciplines have all accomplished 10,000 hours of devoted effort in their discipline. If you look carefully at your own life, you will likely be able to connect the dots. For example, "Stephanie," a person I know, began as an organ player for silent movies. Then she went on to write software programs and compose music using both synthesizers and computers. Upon reflection, Stephanie realized that she had a lifetime of experience with both music and analyzing problems. These hours of experience combined into 10,000 and have led to her composing music for television programs on two continents.

To put it into few words: ***keep learning.***

* * *

To handle risk well involves a multi-faceted approach.

Remember:
- R – reduce the downside
- I – identify the voice of fear and the voice of intuition
- S – set "levels of success"
- K – keep learning

Use both strategy and your deep desire to do something to help you make good decisions about taking appropriate risks. You may not feel comfortable in the middle of risk-taking, but you will likely find a level of fulfillment that is unattainable without stretching yourself.

Good journey to you.

Principle
Reduce the downside, prepare yourself, and pay attention to your "voice of intuition."

Power Questions
What would you attempt if you knew you could not fail? How can your prepare and strengthen yourself so that you're not paralyzed by the fear of failure? What is so important to you that you're willing to devote the study, rehearsal, and preparation so you can achieve it?

* * *

On the topic of risk, we must be proactive. I'll now share insights from Mark Sanborn on being proactive.

6 Things Leaders Forget to Do that Put Them at Risk

by Mark Sanborn, CSP, CPAE

There's much to remember to be a successful leader. Sometimes leaders get so busy and engrossed with day to day operations that they forget some critical remembering activities. Here are six items that need to be on your leadership agenda:

1. Grow a replacement

Your employer can't promote you until they have someone to replace you. You can't move up in the organization if you're the only one who can do that job where you're at right now. And if you're the top boss, you can't let succession planning languish or the fate of your entire organization hangs in the balance.

2. Anticipate problems

Most problems simmer on the back burner before they start to boil over. Like a professional pilot, you've got to be scanning all your instruments and the horizon to make sure you don't get slammed by a potential problem (or at least be completely ready for the problems you can't avoid).

3. Exploit opportunities

Most leaders know what (and who) is wrong, but they become oblivious to opportunities. Who are the star performers who need recognition and development? What are the great opportunities just waiting to be seized? It isn't simple positive/negative thinking: it is about being as focused on the good and opportunistic as you are about the bad and problematic.

4. Change before it is necessary

We all know about the power of disruption and its potential to ruin us. Why it is we wait until the last moment to change? Why not preempt? Staying successful isn't based on your ability to change: it is based on your ability to change faster than your competitors, the needs of your customers and the demands of the marketplace. If you have to change just to keep up, you've lost whatever competitive advantage you could have enjoyed by changing sooner.

5. Stay relevant

What does it even mean to be relevant? Relevancy is about being closely connected: your colleagues, your customer and vendors, and your marketplace. You are deemed relevant when others believes you affect them and their success, and that therefore you and your work matter. In business, customers make the evaluation as to a firm's relevance. What are you doing to stay up-to-date and salient about what matters most to those your lead and serve?

6. Take care of themselves

"Taking care of yourself" seems selfish doesn't it? Maybe that's why so many leaders neglect to do so. Consider: if you're going to model the energy you expect from others, give support and lead the way, you need to be at the top of your game, mentally, emotionally and physically. Burned out leaders burn out followers. The right diet, exercise and rest aren't luxuries but very real necessities for successful leadership.

With so much to do, you need to keep a clear and up to date agenda of the truly important things you consistently need to do. To work without an agenda—and to forget to do the six things above—puts you at risk as a leader.

Mark Sanborn is the president of Sanborn & Associates, Inc., an idea lab for leadership development.

In addition to his experience leading at a local and national level, he has written or co-authored 8 books and is the author of more than two dozen videos and audio training programs on leadership, change, teamwork and customer service. He has presented over 2400 speeches and seminars in every state and a dozen countries.

Mark is a member of the prestigious Speakers Roundtable, 20 of the top speakers in the world today. Mark holds the Certified Speaking Professional (CSP) from the National Speakers Association and is a member of the Speaker Hall of Fame (CPAE).

The author of 8 books, Mark's book, *The Fred Factor: How Passion in Your Work and Life Can Turn the Ordinary Into the Extraordinary* was an international bestseller and has sold over 2 million copies. The sequel, *Fred. 2.0*, was released in March of 2013.

He is the leading authority on turning ordinary into extraordinary and is in demand as a speaker, author and advisor to leaders.

Contact Mark at www.MarkSanborn.com

* * *

One of the insights Mark shared is "change before it is necessary." This really helps. When you're proactive you actually reduce risk!

* * * * * *

USE A SIMPLE, POWERFUL METHOD FOR AMAZING RESULTS
(#6 of the Get Yourself to Take Action)

Want to make a big improvement in your success and fulfillment? Use what I call "The Power of 'Just One.'"

In my 24 books, I have written about thousands of top-level methods and strategies to create more happiness, success and fulfillment in readers' lives. But here is the truth. There are a significant number of people who do not finish reading a book or even a chapter. Worse yet—a number of people simply read about methods but do not even implement *one* new method.

But this is NOT for you.

I invite you to pick Just One action—probably something small and easy—and include it in your daily life.

> *A small daily task, if it be really daily, will beat the labors of a spasmodic Hercules. – Anthony Trollope*

Pick your "Just One."

Here are examples from my clients:
For exercise: 15 minutes on a treadmill
For writing: 250 words a day
For health: add one vegetable to every dinner

Picking and implementing "Just One" helps. It's a cumulative effect. One of my clients does 10 pushups a day. She feels stronger.

Here are 3 Things to Use related to the "Just One" method:

O – open to taking one new action
N – nurture your Autopilot-Coach
E – engage a "Drop-One"

1. Open to taking one new action

As I mentioned above, one new action can yield excellent cumulative results. Author John Grisham said, "If you do not write 1,000 words a day, you're just not serious about writing."

I will suggest a different idea. If one writes 383 words a day, one can still have a draft of a 90,000 word novel in 235 days. That still works, especially for parents who juggle home related-details and going to work. And let's realize that a draft of an entire novel in less than a year is an amazing result. (Another example: a person who goes from sedentary to running a mile a day has created her own personal, amazing result.)

Here's an added bonus. 383 words is easier than 1,000 words, and the writer is following the principle of "Make it a game you can win." For example, I continually exceed my daily writing quota, and that raises my morale.

2. Nurture your Autopilot-Coach

Research data at Stanford University and elsewhere demonstrate that willpower weakens as the day goes on. That's how one can eat a perfect breakfast and then overdo things at dinner time. Watch out for late night eating!

However, you require less energy to meet your goals if you pre-plan your patterns. I often call them a *Positive-Trigger-Pattern.*

For example, my "Just One" action in the morning is based on: "I eat salad for breakfast."

In effect, that phrase jumps into my mind and functions

like my own "Autopilot-Coach." By this I mean, I have a positive, supportive directive that gets me into action. I do not have to make a new decision every morning. Making decisions takes energy. No extra energy is required if I just follow my Autopilot-Coach's suggestion.

Another part of the Autopilot-Coach process is to keep a Progress Log for a "Just One" action. For example, I just noted my daily word count for my novel. Writing down your progress is like hearing a coach say, "Good progress. 15 minutes on the treadmill for today. Well done!"

3. Engage a "Drop-One"

For many of us, our lives are already too full. This is where "Drop One" can help.

For example, from time to time, I drop a number of TV shows off my viewing schedule. I may see the pilot-episode of a TV show, and then immediately decide to "drop it" — that is, I keep the new TV show off my schedule.

Similarly, I may watch one season of a TV show and then drop it. I even stopped watching one season of *The Voice* in the middle of the season. I just was not engaged enough, and I needed the time for more important things.

Another version of "Drop-One" is picking one thing to drop.

My clients have chosen to make these drops:
- I drop the second cookie of the day.
- I drop eating bread.
- I drop calling my brother for support [He just doesn't know how to do that, and I still see him at family gatherings.]

* * *

So remember the Power of "Just One." Pick one new action to integrate into your daily life. Also, consider picking one thing to drop.

The cumulative effects can create amazing results.

This is not merely a theory. I speak from the experiences of writing 24 books, writing screenplays, producing and directing feature films and more.

I've supported clients and graduate students to accomplish great, new things.

I invite you to put "Just One" into effect. When? Today!

Principle

Pick your "Just One" new action and do it daily for great results.

Power Questions

What three possible new actions can make a big difference in your life? Which one feels like it's pulling you to it? Pick something and schedule it.

* * *

Since I mentioned the power of choosing Just One new action, I'll now share Mike Robbins' big insight about an important action, "Be Kind to Yourself."

Be Kind to Yourself
by Mike Robbins
(a lightly edited transcript of a video blog message)

Hey, this is Mike Robbins with another video blog message. This message is all about being kind to ourselves. I posted something on Facebook last week. It was a quote from Brene Brown that said, "Talk to yourself as you would to someone you love."

I was really amazed by the response: lots of posts, lots of shares, lots of likes and lots of people engaging.

As often is the case when I post something that's about being kind, compassionate or loving to ourselves, it seems to really resonate with people. But I notice that, for me and for lots of people I know, the concept of being kind to ourselves, while important and valuable (*and "Yeah, I get it, Amen" and "All right. Absolutely we got to do that; that's so important" and "Put our own oxygen mask on first"*) and all the things that we nod our heads to—it's one thing to understand, but it's a whole other thing to actually do it.

I don't know about you, but I find that being kind to myself, particularly at certain times, is really challenging.

Why is that? What makes it difficult for us to be kind to ourselves?

I think, first of all, a lot of us don't exactly know how to do it. It hasn't been modeled for us. We don't see it a lot around us. If you really think about your life, about the people around you, the culture in which you live, do you know a lot of people [about whom] you can honestly say, "That person is really kind, caring and loving to themselves"?

Or do you see that "this environment is really conducive for me to be kind to myself"? I don't think that's necessarily the case.

I think that we're getting to a point now in certain environments in certain situations where we understand it, at least intellectually. But the practice of it is something completely different.

We have some negative connotations about being kind to yourself. It's seen as self-absorbed or weak. Or "you're going to be kind to yourself; you're going to let yourself off the hook."

Last week, I was having lunch with a friend, who also happens to be a client. He was talking to me about growth-mindset [which is] about having high expectations and high nurturance at the same time. Even though we were talking about this in the context teamwork and leadership and getting the most out of other people, I have been thinking about it in the context our relationship with ourselves.

What if we had really high expectations for ourselves, healthy expectations and really high nurturance? And what's essential to nurturing anyone, including ourselves, is kindness—in addition to empathy, compassion, awareness, and all the other things that go into nurturance.

So it tends to be that we have some resistance to it. I think we're also obsessed with—or we're used to—criticizing ourselves. We've been doing that for years. Many of us have become masters or experts at criticizing ourselves.

The research in social psychology tells us that human beings have between 50,000 and 60,000 separate thoughts every day. On average, eighty percent of those thoughts are negative and critical.

If you're anything like me, and most people I know, most of your thoughts (if you're really honest about it) are about yourself. So eighty percent of our thoughts are negative and critical and most of our thoughts we have everyday are about ourselves, that means the majority of what we're thinking about ourselves is negative. And oftentimes, we speak negatively about ourselves; I mean it's totally socially acceptable to speak negatively about ourselves. We're thinking and saying things that are very critical of ourselves all the time. And this is often the antithesis of kindness.

So what can we do? How can we start to have more kindness for ourselves?

I think the first thing, and it's like with most things, it takes self-awareness. We got to pay attention. We got to notice that we're doing it. What do we do, what we say, how do we act in unkind ways towards ourselves?

Without being critical or judgmental of ourselves, we become aware and see if we can catch ourselves in the act and stop ourselves from being unkind to ourselves. We pay attention to it and have some empathy for ourselves—and then say, "Oh, wait a minute that wasn't very kind. That wasn't very compassionate. That wasn't very accepting and loving towards myself. Let me do or say something different."

At the very least, be aware of doing that and start to pay attention to the impact that it has.

The second thing that we can do once we're aware of it is: it's important that we start to remove the judgment—more specifically, forgive ourselves

Usually we're unkind to ourselves because something specific happened. There's something going on and it's something we're criticizing about ourselves.

So the first thing we have to do is forgive ourselves for whatever it is we're criticizing ourselves for—even if it is genuinely something we don't like, something we want to change, something that we don't deem to be positive. We forgive ourselves for whatever it is.

There's an important distinction between shame and remorse. Shame is about feeling that we're flawed, that we're bad and apparently wrong.

Remorse is about seeing or noticing something about ourselves and feeling badly about [the thing]. Maybe we feel the need to apologize to someone, even to ourselves. [We look] to correct or change or alter behavior. But it doesn't mean that we're bad. So that's the difference. Working with a healthy sense of remorse, we forgive ourselves. Then even more importantly, we forgive ourselves for being critical.

Sometimes I find that I'll forgive myself for whatever it is that I want to change or don't like or think could be altered in some more positive way, but then I have a judgment for myself for being critical in the first place.

It's almost like we're judging the fact that we're judging ourselves, which locks it in. So forgive yourself for what it is, but forgive yourself for being critical of yourself. Because in a lot of places, you know better—just like I do. But that doesn't stop us from doing the judging.

Just because I know better than to eat certain foods or engage in certain activities, that does not mean that I don't do them. [The important thing is to] forgive ourselves for whatever it is, but then more importantly, forgive ourselves for being critical and unkind to ourselves in the first place.

The third thing is to start to practice acts of kindness towards ourselves. Those acts of kindness could look like a lot of different things: saying affirmations, writing in a gratitude journal, taking a walk, breathing, meditating, exercise. A lot of things. There's no list like "here's what to do specifically."

You and I both know how to be kind to other people. Think of a child, a baby, an animal, someone or some thing outside yourself, that it's really easy for you to express kindness for them. You engage with them in kind ways. You don't have to think about it. You don't have to strategize. It's just that "I'm naturally kind with them." Maybe not all the time, but you know what I'm talking about.

What if you could be that way for yourself? What if you could treat yourself with that same level of kindness, that same level of compassion, that same level of love?

Like Brene Brown said, "Talk to yourself as you would to someone you love." That's what self-kindness is all about. And it's an easy, simple concept. It's a simple idea, but it's not always easy to practice. Have compassion with yourself and see if you can start to practice being more kind with yourself. Thanks for watching this video blog message.

Mike Robbins is the author of three books, *Focus on the Good Stuff and Be Yourself, Everyone Else is Already Taken,* and *Nothing Changes Until You Do*. As an expert in teamwork, emotional intelligence, and the powers of appreciation and authenticity, Mike delivers keynote addresses and customized seminars that empower people, teams, and organizations to work together effectively and be more successful. He has inspired tens of thousands of people around the world to reach new levels of awareness and productivity, both personally and professionally. Through his speeches, seminars, and writing, Mike teaches people important techniques that allow them to be more grateful, appreciative, and authentic with others and themselves.

His clients include Google, Wells Fargo, Adobe, Charles Schwab, Twitter, the U.S. Department of Labor, Gap, New York Life, Stanford University, Chevron, eBay, Kaiser, UC Berkeley, Genentech, the San Francisco Giants, and many others. Mike is a member of the National Speakers Association. He has been featured on ABC News, the Oprah radio network, in *Forbes*, the *Washington Post*, and many others. He is a regular contributor to Oprah.com and the Huffington Post. Mike had been drafted by the New York Yankees out of high school. He turned the Yankees down and instead chose to play baseball at Stanford University, where he pitched in the College World Series. Mike was drafted by the Kansas City Royals out of Stanford and played three seasons of professional baseball with the Royals organization before arm injuries ended his playing career while still in the minor leagues.

In addition to earning a degree from Stanford in American Studies with a specialization in race and ethnicity, Mike has extensively studied many disciplines of both personal and professional development, and received training from the Coaches Training Institute.

Mike is a former board member for two non-profit organizations—Challenge Day (a powerful youth organization that focuses on peace, healing, and personal development for teens) and The Peace Alliance (which includes a grassroots political campaign to create a cabinet level U.S. Department of Peace).

In addition to his three books, Mike is also a contributing author to: *Chicken Soup for the Single Parent's Soul, Creating a Marriage You'll Love,* and *Thirty Things to Do When You Turn Thirty*.

Reach Mike at www.mike-robbins.com

BOOK TWO:
YOUR POWER TO LEAP FOWARD AND INCREASE SUCCESS

Power Time Management helps you make exponential improvements in life in addition to graduated improvement. Such change is possible when you're empowered to overcome paralysis and fear. In this section we'll cover these topics:

- Empower Yourself to Handle Disapproval and Rejection
- Power of "The Success Question"
- Power of Harvest Wisdom from a Mistake
- Power of the Next Chapter

EMPOWER YOURSELF TO HANDLE DISAPPROVAL AND REJECTION

Power Time Management is about taking the best actions *without hesitating*.

Unfortunately, two things can cause so much pain that they may paralyze us: disapproval and rejection.

In interviewing successful people, I discovered something surprising: Successful people get rejected more often than others. Why? They *more often* put themselves out into the world where critics reside.

Some of the best college instructors I've met connect with most of their students. However, these dedicated and skillful instructors lament that some students just don't connect with them.

How does this happen? Some students are going through a bumpy patch in life and they withdraw. Other times, personalities just don't mesh well.

So to deal with the sadness of missed opportunities to connect, here's an empowering method:

Use the 30-30-30 Shield

When asked how she deals with a lot of pressure (as pro athlete, *Sports Illustrated* model, mother and wife of celebrity surfer Laird Hamilton), Gabrielle Reese said, **"In life, you will always have 30 percent of the people who love you, 30 percent who hate you and 30 percent who couldn't care less."**

We can use the above quote as part of what I call a "30-30-30 Shield." How?

The ideas of Gabrielle's quote release us from trying to be

perfect and from trying to please everyone.

Many of us experience a huge drop in energy and motivation when under-fire by others' criticism.

Your first thoughts might be on the order of: "Oh, no! I can't do anything right. Nobody's going to like [my book, my blog, my artwork, etc.]."

Instead, invoke your 30-30-30 Shield.

You can assess: "Is this person part of the 30 percent who will never understand the value of what I'm doing? Are they someone who will never care? If so, I can dismiss them from my mind."

With the above, you could even "shield" your self-esteem. When someone slams criticism at us, it can feel like a blow to our self-esteem.

But with the 30-30-30 Shield we can assess: "This person just doesn't care about what I care about." or "Evidently, I made artwork that does not appeal to this person. I'll serve my own audience."

We can devote more time to thinking about the 30% who do love us:

Being deeply loved by someone gives you strength, while loving someone deeply gives you courage. – Lao Tzu.

In summary, guide your own thoughts. Don't let them fall into a negative spiral. Instead, employ your 30-30-30 Shield and rejoice in being fully alive. You experiment with creativity, take appropriate risks and concentrate on those people who can relate to your style of creativity.

* * *

As mentioned, successful people prepare to take risks and

to face disapproval and rejection.

To go further with this topic, I'll now introduce two valuable methods:

a) Reduce the downside
b) Reduce emotional pain

A. Reduce the Downside

The downside is anything that can go wrong that will cause you pain and trouble. We'll use the P.I.N. process to help you prepare. When you feel prepared, you'll save time that would have been lost to fear and paralysis.

P – plan the "budget"
I – identify worst case scenarios and "remedies"
N – nurture yourself through it

(I use the word "P.I.N." as a reminder to pinpoint crucial details.)

1. Plan the "budget"

When you have a "budget," you can make a solid plan so that you won't "lose the store." That is, you avoid having everything come crashing down. The budget that I refer to includes money, time and effort.

Every book I write has a budget. I learned from one of my mentors, Marc Allen, publisher of *The Power of Now*, that one has to be careful to avoid spending too much on any particular book, or the company will fail to make a profit.

Without careful planning, I will not have the funds to devote to more projects. So I'm sure to identify each budget. For example, for this book, my time budget focused on making the book around 202 pages long. Years ago, I wrote books at 390 and 420 page lengths. I discovered that those books did not sell better than a 202 pages long book.

I have adjusted my time budgets accordingly.

2. Identify worst case scenarios and "remedies"

When you identify the worst things that can go wrong, and you come up with solutions or "remedies," you feel prepared and strong.

For example, I guide my college-level, public-speaking students, to write up a list of *10 Questions I Do Not Want to Answer*. Then I guide them to come up with two answers for each terrible question. Once they complete this process, they're prepared! They feel stronger and they can respond better to tough questions (even ones that were not part of their list).

3. Nurture yourself through it

Let's face it. Many of us will hesitate or avoid doing a project altogether if we anticipate that it will "hurt too much." That's the reason that it's good to have a plan of how you'll nurture yourself through the whole process.

One element that helps me is that I gather a team for each book. I have editors and even someone who will listen to me read the first draft of each section of the book.

Further, I space out the work. I may write 400 words a day. I write in the morning, and the rest of the day may be devoted to work or recreation.

What can you do to nurture yourself so that you're strong and can endure (and even enjoy) the journey of a long project?

B. Reduce Emotional Pain

When things do not turn out as planned, it hurts. The question is whether a person falls into behaviors to avoid such pain or not.

An Effective Method for Dealing with Rejection: "Celebrate Someone Disagrees"

Recently, a friend who is an author gave a speech to a small group. No one purchased his books. He told me later, "Tom, you would have sold books."

Trying to reduce his pain, I replied, "You had a tough crowd. Besides, the topics of my books are different."

This did not help. So I just supported him by saying, "How are you going Celebrate Someone Disagrees?"

Now, I had shared this "Celebrate Someone Disagrees" idea with Joe before. In essence, this idea means that you don't let fear stop you. You do what you hope to do and what you plan to do, knowing that someone is not going to like your work, your ideas, your expression of your feelings, or something else.

When someone says "I don't like your book" (which can be expressed by no one buying a copy), it simply hurts.

The question is about how you grieve, when you grieve and how much of your time it takes up.

I support grieving. When a close friend killed himself, I grieved. I even choked up when in front of a classroom of graduate students.

However, today, I don't grieve as long each day.

The idea of "Celebrate Someone Disagrees" is about acknowledging that someone disagrees about the value that you're offering *and still* you celebrate:
- Your courage in putting something into the world
- Your standing up and saying to the world, "This is what I can do now. Sure, I'll probably improve or at least change my work in the future."

- Your persistence in finishing a project! You're a "completer."

Back to my friend Joe.

When I said, "How are you going to Celebrate Someone Disagrees?"

He burst into a smile and said, "Ice cream."

Celebrate Someone Disagrees does not replace grieving.

Instead, think of it as a pleasant and powerful element that you add!

* * *

When you employ Power Time Management, you move ahead quickly. You'll take appropriate risks. Remember to use your 30-30-30 Shield and the "Celebrate Someone Disagrees" process.

Principle

When you prepare well to handle disapproval and rejection, you're strong and you can take appropriate risks — and truly succeed.

Power Questions

What will you identify as elements of your own "Celebrate Someone Disagrees" process? How will you remind yourself to take appropriate risks and to employ your "30-30-30 Shield"?

* * * * * *

POWER OF "THE SUCCESS QUESTION"
(#2 of Increase Success)

To get more done in less time and to do what will most benefit your personal success, you need empowering answers to one question: "Are you ready to succeed?"

Here's a second question: **"Every day are you training, rehearsing and studying so that you are ready to jump at opportunity?"**

This means so much to me that I read 85 books a year. I also have a number of mentors.

This ability to be ready has meant a lot to my life.

Several years ago, I was co-producing and directing a feature film. We were able to get a small budget together but not a budget that could afford a particular lead actor.

My co-producer turned to me and asked, "Tom, why don't you play that part?"

My first response was: "I'm already directing. That's a lot of work." But soon after, I said, "Yes!" I'm glad that I responded with "Yes."

Can You Say "Yes" to the Big Challenges?

How could I say "Yes" to both starring in and directing a feature film? It's because I had trained as an actor. I had acted in a number of short films, and I had acting mentors.

* * *

Later, I gave a speech to help people out of work learn to effectively gain jobs.

A person came up to me and said, "You should be a speaker at [xy] company."

I replied, "Who do I talk with?"

The man told me.

"Do you have your cell phone? How about you leave a voicemail for her?" I asked.

I knew that the man's positive feelings about me were at their peak so I guided him to leave a message in that moment.

That one discussion led to work that totaled more than $235,000.

In three sentences, I guided someone to help me get connected to a valuable opportunity.

How did I do that?

I was ready!

Now, I'll guide you through the Y.E.S. process

Y – yearn for knowledge and experience
E – energize yourself
S – set up rehearsal

1. Yearn for knowledge and experience

Remember my earlier question: ***"Every day are you training, rehearsing and studying so that you are ready to jump at opportunity?"***

To be ready, you must prepare every day. You never know when an opportunity will present itself.

We simply do not have the time to make a bunch of mistakes. By studying and reading, you can learn from those who have achieved much. You can avoid the mistakes that they have gone through. You'll save time. You'll do better than you would have done without the knowledge.

Also, get training. Practice. Some years ago, I practiced negotiating by going to a flea market and negotiating over the price of books. Beyond that practice, I kept track of what

I learned in several negotiations over the years and wrote a book, *Darkest Secrets of Negotiation Masters*.

Stay on a continuing quest to improve your skills.

2. Energize yourself

Enough sleep, exercise, and good nutrition form a solid foundation for your success. Without energy, you cannot confidently and powerfully say YES! to opportunities when they appear. When you want to improve something, measure it. For example, some of my clients log their sleep hours. I emphasize: *Don't guess. Measure for Success.*

3. Set up rehearsal

When my clients and college level public speaking students complete rehearsal sessions, I can tell in their performance, and I praise them for their good work. When they have not done five days of 9-minute Rehearsals, I can notice that, too. And so can the audience!

Ideally, you complete a 9-minute Rehearsal session in the morning. Why? Then your subconscious mind can work on the material throughout the day.

Use the Y.E.S. process so that you're *ready* for surprise opportunities.

Take your life to a higher level—faster.

Principle

Prepare, study, read and rehearse every day so that you're *ready* to succeed.

Power Questions

What will you do today to give yourself an advantage? What will you rehearse or study or read?

* * *

Since I mentioned the above "success question" of *Are your ready to succeed?*, now I'll share Randy Gage's powerful point about readiness and really succeeding.

Be Electric!
by Randy Gage
(a lightly edited transcript of a video episode)

Hey, everybody. Welcome to another episode of Prosperity TV. I'm Randy Gage. I'm actually coming to you from my place here in South Beach. I want to talk about electricity, or more specifically, I want to talk about energy — how you have more energy for success.

Here's what I would share with you. It was probably about 15 years ago, and I came to a realization. I thought, "You know, I'm kind of a smart guy. I figured out some things. I've learned some lessons about business. I've learned some marketing stuff, some stuff about success. But I'm never going to be rich if I don't get my health back. [That is,] if I don't get energy to attack some of these great ideas that I have, I'm never going to be successful.

That realization was a big turnaround for me, and it can be a big turnaround point for you as well. Because here's the thing about energy: Most people talk about "I don't have any energy and I can't find any energy."

You don't find energy. You don't have energy. What the most successful people have learned is you *create* energy! Your body is this internal combustion engine. It's this most brilliant piece of engineering you'll ever find anywhere. I mean, take the most advanced programming of the most advanced computer, the most advanced machine. Now put it next to the human body, and it pales in comparison.

The trillions of cells you have in the heart pumping, in the blood flowing, in the liver doing its job, in the pancreas. And in mobility and in eyesight, in hearing and the impulses from the brain. This machine is amazing.

But you know what you control? [It's] how much energy it creates. Now, how do you do that? Let's talk about the food you eat or don't. By the things you drink or don't drink. By the addictions you participate in or choose not to participate in. By the exercise you practice or don't practice.

All of those things are all things that you have control over. When you feed your body the right food, the right liquid, you move it around. You keep it away from dangerous, deadly, poisonous, toxic things.

And [you stay away from] dangerous, poisonous, toxic people. [I've shared a couple of videos about dealing with negative people] so I will not belabor that point this week.

I really just want to talk about how we create energy with [good, nutritious] food and drinking lots of fresh water.

Let's throw in sleep: The sleep you get or don't get.

You control those things and that's how you create energy. When you have energy, it's amazing what you can accomplish.

And please get the word out about Prosperity TV to the loved ones in your life. Let's spread this message for Prosperity.

Until next week, Peace. I love you, guys.

(End of this lightly edited transcript.)

Randy Gage is the author of nine books, including the *New York Times* bestseller, *Risky Is the New Safe*. He has spoken in 48 U.S. States, all Canadian provinces and 48 other countries, to more than 2 million people. He was listed in the "Who's Hot" article for *Speaker Magazine* and in 2013 was inducted into the Speakers Hall of Fame.

www.RandyGage.com

Prosperity TV at http://www.youtube.com/randygage

* * *

Since we talked about getting your body in good health so you're ready to succeed, now let's learn Cheryl Wood's insights about empowering your mind.

The Power of Sizzle
by Cheryl Wood

"Your ultimate success and ability to create your own Sizzle in life is defined by your thoughts. Every day, choose thoughts that are positive and progressive, and witness the shift in your life."
– Cheryl Wood

So, what is Sizzle? Sizzle is the unique space you carve out for yourself in the world and the un-duplicable mark you leave based on your gifts and talents that no one can take from you. That means, every person reading this book has The Power to SIZZLE.

Truthfully, as a young, African-American girl raised in poverty in the projects of Baltimore City, the product of a single-parent household, I never expected to have the word "Sizzle" show-up in my life. If anything, I expected just the opposite. As I observed my surroundings growing up— mostly crime, violence, poverty, and lack of educational resources—I presumed I was destined for very little success in my life. But the one glimmer of hope came from a woman I respected as the epitome of belief: my mother. Her constant belief that things would work out, that she could somehow create a solution to every challenge she faced, and the fortitude that she did not have to become a product of her environment moved me to start believing I had a choice in the type of life I could create for myself.

I never saw my mother cave into the pressure she clearly faced as a single mother raising three young children on a minimal salary as a public school cafeteria manager. I never saw her express disgust or lack of willpower to find solutions even when she didn't know how she was going to feed us, pay a utility bill, afford school clothes, or pay for repairs to our used, barely-running Chevrolet Nova that took us to and from "only the necessary" places.

My mother was (and still is) by far one of the most inspirational women in my life. She instilled in me hope that thru hard work, persistence, determination, loyalty, and trustworthiness, I could accomplish anything. She was the first female influence in my life who taught me the power of shifting my thoughts to create the reality I wanted.

And, now, as a mother myself I instill that same training in my three children so they understand the power they have to become, do, or accomplish anything they put their minds to. It's so true that shifting your mindset can shift your life. And the only way to shift your mindset is to shift your thoughts. Your thoughts can either motivate and energize you to get what you want in life or hinder you and keep you stuck where you are right now in life. Granted, that's not to say that because you start thinking positive thoughts right now that your goals, aspirations and dreams will miraculously come to fruition tomorrow.

Let's face it, you have to put in the work for what you say you want. And reaching the stars is going to require a lot of climbing. It takes time to SIZZLE. It's a process like anything else. And it's a daily journey that will have highs and lows. But the guarantee is that as you shift your thoughts to POWER thoughts—positive, empowering thoughts that refuel you to keep pushing towards your big dream—you will become more determined than ever not to throw in the towel. One of the best pieces of advice I ever heard was, "You only fail when you stop trying." (Bob Marley)

As you delve into the POWER Thoughts I share in this article, allow each thought to sink-in and transform who you are, how you think, and what you believe you can accomplish!

- **POWER Thought #1**

If you really want to achieve success and prosperity you must add Persistence to your Prayers, Follow Through to your Faith, Intention to your Inspiration, and Movement to your Motivation. Nothing will happen until you persistently follow through on your intentions and make constant moves towards pursuing what you say you want.

- **POWER Thought #2**

Stop waiting for validation or permission. No other individual and no amount of accolades can convince you that you are good enough—that's an inside job. It's all on YOU! Repeat this on a daily basis because you deserve to create your own reality then grant yourself permission to dream bigger, play bigger, and expect to achieve the results you work hard for.

- **POWER Thought #3**

Regardless of how many conferences, workshops, or training sessions you attend, how many thousands of dollars you spend on learning products, and how many coaches you hire... until you firmly believe in your gifts and EXECUTE on what's already in your arsenal you will keep getting the same results. Starting today, utilize what you already have and know to get unstuck.

- **POWER Thought #4**

Repeatedly ask yourself: Do I choose to be held hostage by fear or will I permit myself to be enlightened by hope and possibilities? Your possibilities in life will be as big as you make room for. Stop playing small!

- **POWER Thought #5**

To get what you want, you have to know what you want. To know what you want you have to clearly identify it by writing it down. Any goal or ambition not written down is just a wish. Take out your notepad and pen and start writing about the reality you want to create for your life.

- **POWER Thought #6**

Everything is not meant for everyone. Don't get sidetracked by the "hype" of what everyone else is doing. Stop and make sure your dreams and the work you're putting in align with YOUR vision of success. It is much more rewarding, fulfilling and enjoyable to run your own race at your own pace.

- **POWER Thought #7**

Your success depends on your willingness to frequently assess what you've been doing, acknowledge what you need to change, and execute to change it!

Cheryl Wood is a compelling thought leader and motivational speaker who possesses a deep-seated passion for supporting the personal development and economic empowerment of women globally. Cheryl has impacted the lives of thousands of women through her life-changing principles of FEARLESS living and inspires women to embrace their personal power to create the life they want. Her personal story is one of persistence and resilience as a mother of three who transitioned from a t-shirt business in her basement to growing an international speaking and coaching business. She is an award-winning entrepreneur, speaker, author, and business coach who has been spotlighted on Fox 5 News, News Channel 8, Radio One, and *Afro-American Newspaper*, to name a few.

Cheryl has received numerous awards and recognition for her work including the 2014 Success In Stilettos Award, 2013 Willie Jolley Motivational Speaker Award, 2012 Forty Under 40 Small Business Honoree, and 2012 Inspirational Entrepreneur of the Year Award, among others.

She has authored three books: *How I Flatlined and Woke Up in 45 Days—A Guide to Empowered Living*; *The GlamourLESS Side of Entrepreneurship, What They DIDN'T Tell You About Being A Woman In Business*; and *The Power to Sizzle: Transformational Power Thoughts for Creating the Life You Want*. The excerpt above is from her most recent book, *The Power to Sizzle*. All three books can be purchased on Amazon.com.

For more information:
Visit www.cherylwoodempowers.com
Contact: info@cherylwoodempowers.com

* * * * * *

POWER OF HARVESTING WISDOM FROM A MISTAKE
(#3 of Increase Success)

Imagine if you had a way to reduce your fear and assure yourself that you'll be okay even if you make a significant mistake. Several years ago, I wrote about the Solution-for-Error Plan in my book *Be Heard and Be Trusted*.

Now I want to revisit the Plan because it has a significant relevance to Power Time Management in that you'll save time, and your next efforts will be more productive.

Solution-for Error Plan

What if you had no fear of making mistakes? Would you try more things? Would your career take a leap forward?

Great communicators are effective because they take action, learn, and improve through feedback. If you do nothing, you cannot improve.

My clients use the Solution-for-Error Plan to gain these terrific benefits:

- Live an extraordinary life
- Remove self-defeating patterns
- Eliminate guilt feelings

You can live an extraordinary life

Top achievers who experience deep satisfaction and fulfillment have effectively learned how to stretch themselves, make mistakes, and learn so they can improve their performance.

The secret is that when we make a mistake, we quickly learn from it and do better. This is the reason I have developed the Solution-for-Error process.

An error doesn't become a mistake until you refuse to correct it.
— Orlando A. Battista

I have missed more than 9,000 shots in my career. I have lost almost 300 games. On 26 occasions I have been entrusted to take the game winning shot, and I missed. And I have failed over and over and over again in my life. And that is precisely why I succeed.
— Michael Jordan

Anyone who doesn't make mistakes isn't trying hard enough.
— Wess Roberts

The people who take leaps forward in their lives engage in calculated risks. An old phrase says, "The person who never makes a mistake always takes orders from one who does." I have seen the value of this idea from talking with highly effective people. Entrepreneurs, and company presidents take calculated risks. They have employees who keep their heads down and seek only security. These employees prefer to accomplish routine tasks.

Creativity is allowing yourself to make mistakes.
Art is knowing which ones to keep. - Scott Adams

Researchers note that society provides big rewards to people who express their creativity and natural brilliance. Producers, actors, presidents, CEOs, and entrepreneurs are rewarded with astronomical salaries, bonuses, and residual income.

The idea is to harvest wisdom from your experiences. Think of the old phrase, "Good judgment comes from experience. Experience often comes from bad judgment." Let's harvest wisdom from our own experiences.

The Solution-for-Error Plan helps us to impact our subconscious minds quickly and powerfully with the lessons we need to learn so that we experience deep understanding. In this way, we empower ourselves.

When I did [the feature film] 1941, I felt I was made of Teflon. I felt that anything I put on film was going to succeed. I felt invincible. And in a sense, at that point in my life, the best thing that could have happened was the drubbing that 1941 got both from the critics and the public... I sobered up so quickly. [On 1941] I had gotten so precious... I should have had a second unit film the Ferris wheel [miniature special effects ... I was taking 20 takes on simple insert shots]. I couldn't let go. I couldn't share the workload with anyone. And I learned the greatest lessons of my career just from the experience of 1941... I went from the disaster of 1941 to my first day of shooting on Raiders *[of the Lost Ark]. In a sense, Raiders rescued me from getting self-involved with 'Oh dear, the movie is going to be a failure and all the critics will hate it'... By the time I did* Raiders*, I was humbled. Every shot was storyboarded. I was 14 days under schedule...* Raiders of the Lost Ark *was probably the most prepared I have ever been in my career to direct a movie, and it paid off. – Steven Spielberg*

I noticed that my clients felt limitations because of certain ideas they had read in books. Those books included good ideas, but the ideas were not integrated and hands-on. Many books do not give us a way to play with the material and feel it. Again and again, I've noticed people communicating lovely ideas that were merely rationally-oriented. To make massive progress, you need to feel it. As James Brown sang many years ago, "I feel good!"

With this insight, I developed the Solution-for-Error Plan to overcome the limitations that can arise in people from their mere reading of ideas in books.

Remove self-defeating patterns

Would your life leap forward to more enjoyment and greater success if you could break your self-defeating patterns? The Solution-for-Error Plan helps us pay attention to what went wrong and how to fix it.

For novice salespeople, self-defeating behaviors include devoting too little time to study and rehearsal, and then winging it. Winging it often leads to missed sales. Top producers study, rehearse their presentations and close more sales. With the Solution-for-Error Plan, we identify beneficial behaviors that can lead to breakthroughs.

Eliminate guilt feelings

How much lighter would you feel if you could eliminate guilt feelings?

The Solution-for-Error Plan helps us quickly develop a game plan for doing better. It is a planning process that allows us to escape from the endless loop of vague guilt feelings. Through this process, we can identify ineffective behaviors and focus on correcting them. We can say, "Okay, I blew it that time, but now I know how I can do better next time."

Psychologists have pointed out that punishment can often be ineffective because it only stops a behavior without providing productive alternative behavior. The Solution-for-Error Plan helps us identify the solutions, or productive alternative behaviors, so that we feel relieved and empowered.

You always pass failure on the way to success.
— Mickey Rooney

Nobody has a problem; it's only a decision waiting to be made. If my so-called "problem" is the result of a bad decision that I made yesterday, then all I have to do is make another decision—a better decision—today! — Robert H. Schuller

As a general rule the most successful man in life is the man who has the best information. — Benjamin Disraeli

Some of the best information only becomes available when you take action and discover how you function in new and challenging situations. You learn where your natural brilliance is and which areas you need to improve. You may also learn that it is better to delegate certain tasks to people who have a natural talent in an area in which you do not excel.

A discovery is said to be an accident meeting a prepared mind.
— Albert von Szent Gyorgyi

Many of the most successful people have noted that we learn more from a mistake or failure than from a successful outcome. The Solution-for-Error Plan helps you squeeze any experience and get the learning from it. You learn from what went wrong so you can correct it.

Failure is success if we learn from it. — Malcolm Forbes

Soon, I will show you the form that my company uses. We dare to achieve; occasionally, therefore, a situation turns out in a disappointing manner. The point is to learn, plan a better approach for future action and move on.

You miss 100% of the shots you don't take.
- Wayne Gretzky

It's better to explore life and make mistakes than to play it safe. Mistakes are part of the dues one pays for a full life.
- Sophia Loren

What if a 10-minute method could help you squeeze an experience or tough situation and learn what you need to learn from it? That method is the Solution-for-Error Plan.

Let's go into action and learn the Solution-for-Error Plan from this fictional example.

Solution-for-Error Plan (example)

Step 1: What's the error and what led to it?

Started a business with another person, with whom I did not develop a full written agreement. We were friends. We trusted each other as friends and thought that we were compatible as business partners.

What were the painful consequences, or the feelings you want to avoid?

It broke my heart when I found that I could not rely on my business partner to carry the ball when I was tired. I felt abandoned. Finally, the business was failing because it needed both of us to have full dedication in the startup phase.

Step 2 How can you avoid the error? What can you do better?

I can (a) study what I need in a business partner, (b) hold a number of meetings with any potential partner, (c) hire a well-respected consultant to help assess whether we are compatible as business partners, and (d) write a full agreement, including an exit strategy.

Step 3 How can you compensate for your own tendency?

My tendency is to jump right in and not take time to look at all potential problems. I can compensate for that tendency by hiring someone (who is highly recommended) to walk through the potential consequences with me.

Step 4 What did you do right?

I took action. I learned what does *not* work for me. Now that I know what my tendencies can create, I can be careful in similar situations.

Step 5 What does the solution look like? What does it feel like?

I gain the right business partner, whom I can trust. My ideal is the partnership of Walt Disney and his brother, Roy O. Disney.

Step 6 What are the benefits of the solution to you? To the team?

I will save myself from heartache and stress. With the right business partner, my quality of life will improve. I won't have to stay at the office all the time. I'll have time for my family. My team will feel better and be more productive when I am not stressed out.

Step 7 How can you reward yourself for taking action?

I will make relaxation appointments for myself: time for reading, taking hot baths, and walking in nature.

* * *

Now let us investigate the Solution-for-Error Plan in greater detail.

What's the Error and What Led to It?
I chose the word error with care. As we noted earlier,

An error doesn't become a mistake until you refuse to correct it.
– Orlando A. Battista

The first step is to face up to the error. We must acknowledge that we had something to do with the situation. We need to pay close attention to the details of what happened and then write down the error. Write what caused you to feel bad or what action you failed to take. For example, a workshop participant wrote, "I allowed myself to get tired, so that I was irritable later." Many people respect the one who admits an error and says, "With what I know now, here is my new plan … "

What led to the error?
Note the steps that led to the error. They may be something like staying up too late, or procrastinating on

doing research to prepare for a first meeting with a potential client.

What were the painful consequences or feelings I want to avoid?

Identify the feelings related to the error that you want to avoid. For example, "I want to avoid feeling angry"; "I want to avoid feeling wronged"; or "I want to avoid feeling ignored." You can begin the process of dropping these feelings when you write them down in your Solution-for-Error Plan.

To create behavior change, we often need to stop and become aware of the price we have paid for the error. We need to recognize the error's consequences. The consequence of an error can be, "I feel that I failed the job interview because I didn't prepare beforehand by studying the company."

The good news is that as soon as you identify the error and what led to it, you have power that you didn't have moments before. You can take action from this moment onward to do better in life.

Now you're ready for the next question.

How Can You Avoid the Error? What Can You do Better?

Fear is the father of courage and the mother of safety.
– Henry H. Tweedy

Errors frequently occur because we didn't do something or we didn't prepare for a situation. We need to take preventative, proactive steps, which are like preventative medicine. This is proactive: you need to go out there and do it first, to prevent negative consequences from happening.

Consider every mistake you do make as an asset.
– Paul J. Meyer

Many of us remember procrastinating on a school paper until the night before it was due. Then we berated ourselves, telling ourselves, "I'll never let it get this bad again." Does this sound familiar? Does it remind you of how you prepare the paperwork for your taxes?

With the Solution-for-Error Plan, you'll have a powerful incentive to avoid letting this happen again, because you're going to remember how much pain the error caused. Also, you'll remember all the good things you can create in your life by taking proactive steps. You will have leverage on yourself in both directions: pain and joy (or pleasure).

An important component of this step is to note due dates for your proactive steps.

What can we do better?

In order to do better, we often need a team. In a team of people, one person can compensate for another's shortcoming.

Sometimes it helps to have a post-game review. For example, one friend told me about an error he experienced during a memorial service. A group of people gathered on a 70-foot yacht for the spreading of ashes in the ocean. Later, my friend told me, "I wasn't thinking straight. The grief had distracted me. If I was thinking clearly, I would have asked my wife to wear a life-jacket. No one wore life-jackets. Fortunately, no one fell over the side, even though the ocean was rough."

My friend was concerned about his oversight. He told me, "I am repeating this story to you so I learn the lesson."

Learning the lesson is the purpose of answering the question, "How can you avoid the error? What can we do better?"

How Can You Compensate for Your Own Tendency?

Harvest wisdom from an error and you are twice blessed: you won't repeat the error and you know what to compensate for.
– Tom Marcoux

Know your tendencies and compensate for them. People who accomplish more and feel inner peace have a different perspective on the mistakes they make. They understand that life is constantly offering us lessons. If we don't learn the lessons, the opportunities for learning (what we call our "problems") are repeated until we learn to take effective action. So we do well when we learn to compensate for a troublesome personal tendency.

To compensate is to make a correction. A salesperson may talk too much, leave out a detail, forget to ask for the sale, or miss the chance to engage a new person in conversation (and miss the resulting referrals). This salesperson can compensate by turning each mistake around. If he or she talks too much, the turn around is to listen more.

In your personal journal, write down some of your mistakes and find the turn around for each mistake. You'll make surprising progress when you follow through with this process.

What Did You Do Right?

A balanced view of our actions often reveals that we did something right. This section reminds us that certain behavior patterns *are still* valuable.

Sometimes we take the right action and something still

doesn't work. Perhaps the interviewer was feeling ill, so the meeting went poorly in spite of our preparation. We don't always know. In any case, we need to keep up our morale by acknowledging our correct efforts.

Buckminster Fuller, who was considered a genius, emphasized the value of learning from mistakes:

If I ran a school, I'd give the average grade to the ones who gave me all the right answers, for being good parrots. I'd give the top grades to those who made a lot of mistakes and told me about them, and then told me what they learned from them.
– Buckminster Fuller

Constant effort and frequent mistakes are the stepping stones of genius. – Elbert Hubbard

[For my first album, Virgin Records] gave me no budget— practically no budget. I said "Prince, I will choreograph for you for free; you write me a song"... I worked with Kool and the Gang— [and I said] I need rhythm tracks; for your next tour [I'll choreograph for you]. I would go on and on, and I would barter deals... – Paula Abdul

Paula Abdul's first album was a big success, due in large part to the quality she gained with her bartered deals. But during her successful career as a popular music icon, she was not immune to feelings of self-doubt.

[I had] the real scary feeling of "Oh, no, I'm a fraud. I'm just waiting for them to find out. Fraud, fraud, fraud, fraud." Because I never knew that everyone else does the same thing. You end up becoming who you are by actually jumping into that circle of fear

and doing it. And that's how you end up believing in yourself.
– Paula Abdul

We learn from Paula that the process is about doing and learning as you go.

We do not wait for the absence of fear. We use fear to help us learn what we need to do better.

This reminds me of how persistent Randy Pausch was in pursuing his childhood goal of becoming an Imagineer. He pushed beyond the first rejection letters that came to him from Walt Disney Imagineering. He continued in his efforts and eventually worked with Walt Disney Imagineering on Disney's *Aladdin*. Randy said:

The brick walls are there for a reason: they are there to give us a chance to show how badly we want something. Because the brick walls are there to stop those people who don't want it badly enough.... If you lead your life the right way, the karma will take care of itself, the dreams will come to you.
– Dr. Randy Pausch

When we focus on what we did right, we often discover that we can feel good about some of our efforts. With this encouragement, we have the energy to refine our approach for the next occasion.

What Does the Solution Look /Feel Like?
If we think happy thoughts we will be happy. If we think miserable thoughts, we will be miserable. – Dale Carnegie

Identify what you can do that will prevent a similar error from occurring in the future. Perhaps you can rehearse or write out your sales pitch. You might find that exercising or changing your diet will provide you with more energy. These are actions you can use to replace self-defeating actions.

What are you going to get after you change your behavior? Are you going to serve more people, make more money, win an award or earn a vacation in Hawaii? You can use the Solution-for-Error Plan for every area of your life. You can use it to enhance your personal and business relationships.

Ask yourself, "What do I want to feel?" One client wrote, "I want to feel connected. I want to feel on course with my purpose." Often we want to feel powerful, strong, healthy, and joyful. It is crucial to target the feelings you want that the Solution can provide. You can feel prosperous, successful, and good about yourself.

What are the Benefits of the Solution?
Possible benefits, to you, to the team:
- I feel closer to my loved one.
- I have great job interviews.
- I feel relaxed.
- I feel the tension drain from my shoulders.
- I feel at peace more often during the day.

Here's an example of a valuable benefit, noted in this e-mail message from a client:

Tom, I had another social success after applying some of the techniques I learned in your workshop and book. I am on the social committee here at work. We had our company Thanksgiving lunch and Potluck last Thursday. I was on the decorating committee, and as it turned out, ended up being the hostess as well. As people brought in the food, they started asking me where to put things, and—Well, I ended up directing things. There was one moment of panic. I had left for a few minutes, to wash my hands and as I came back I heard the roar of voices. The room had been filling up in my absence, and the voices seemed to reach a deafening volume (anxiety attack), but I took a deep breath, told myself this was an improvisation of a party-scene where I was the confident hostess, and walked in. I used your method of "Act as if." Someone came up to me to ask if there was anything that still needed to be done, and that helped me get started directing things once again. Thanks Tom, for helping me through another tricky situation.

My client acted as if she were a confident hostess. With more practice, she is likely to find that she eventually feels like a confident hostess.

You gain strength, courage, and confidence by every experience in which you really stop to look fear in the face. You must do the thing you think you cannot do. – Eleanor Roosevelt

When you focus on the real benefit, you feel the energy to take an appropriate risk. We need to remember to take action in the manner of a person who believes in himself or herself. When start to trust yourself, other people follow along and trust you, too.

How Can you Reward Yourself for Taking Action?

What tangible reward will you immediately present to yourself for changing your own behavior? I call this a self-reward. For example, I sometimes associate the purchase of a book with the successful accomplishment of a specific action. During my seminars, audience members suggest self-rewards such as a warm bath, reading a book, and getting a neck massage.

A special form of reward

The power to transcend fear comes from our burning desire and intense interest in doing the actual work. The work itself needs to be intrinsically enjoyable and valuable to us.

If you think that the finished book is of greater value than what you learned from the writing process, you are mistaken.
— Terry Brooks

If you don't think there is magic in writing, you probably won't write anything magical. — Terry Brooks

Many people would like to have written a book. But the effective writers I know *like to write*. Find what you like doing.

Principle

Use the Solution-for-Error Plan to help you learn and move on.

Power Question

If you knew that you could not fail, what would you attempt? (If you learn from each experience, there is no failure.)

On the next page, find a blank copy of the Solution-for-Error Plan form for your repeated use.

Solution-for-Error Plan

Step 1. What's the error and what led to it? What are the painful consequences, or the feelings you want to avoid?

Step 2. How can you avoid the error? What can you do better?

Step 3. How can you compensate for your own tendency?

Step 4. What did you do right?

Step 5. What does the solution look like? What does it feel like?

Step 6. What are the benefits of the solution to you? To the team?

Step 7. How can you reward yourself for taking action?

© Tom Marcoux   Tom's blog: BeHeardandBeTrusted.com

POWER OF THE NEXT CHAPTER
(#4 of the Increase Success)

Imagine that you could jump ahead in life. There are times when it requires letting go of something that is precious to you.

We must be willing to let go of the life we planned so as to have the life that is waiting for us. – Joseph Campbell

When I directed my first feature film, I thought it would immediately lead to directing several films in a row. The film did okay. No big, huge response.

I didn't let this lack of response hold me back. Instead, I explored various creative roads, writing 24 books, guest-lecturing at Stanford University, composing music, speaking to audiences at IBM, Sun Microsystems, Silicon Valley Bank and more. Further, I turned my storytelling skills to writing three graphic novels and a text-novel of my *Jack AngelSword* franchise.

Through my experiences, I learned to embrace "the life that was waiting for me." I'm glad I did!

* * *

Then there is another side to life: Many of us have experienced dark, horrible times that have left us feeling scarred, scared and stuck. Several years ago, I led a book project. At that time, I met a contributing author, "Claire." Claire was a psychotherapist who had a severely painful past. She had been brutally raped, but she told me: "That was the first chapter of my life. It's part of the book of my life. **But I'm in the second chapter now."**

Claire's declaration of being in a second chapter has always remained in my thoughts. She was determined *not* to remain stuck. She also did *not* deny the extreme impact of the horrific event. But she became an advocate for women and their healing.

When one door of happiness closes, another opens; but often we look so long at the closed door that we do not see the one which has been opened for us. – Helen Keller

You can save time by using a phrase as your pivot point. You might say, **"That was then. I'm in my new chapter now."**

If something positive ends but you're having trouble letting go, you might tell yourself, **"That was a good run."**

By using that phrase, you can be grateful for the "good run," and still you can appreciate the new "open door." You can step forward into your new chapter and *the life that is waiting for you.*

Principle

You can benefit from a new chapter of life, *and* it might require letting go of the life you've planned. But it's worth it.

Power Questions

What opportunities are present for you now? Do you need to let go of an old role or an old regret? Would you like to welcome a new chapter of your life?

* * *

Since we have been talking about opportunities, here are Patricia Fripp's insights about opportunities and how to make the most of them.

Opportunity Does Not Knock Once
by Patricia Fripp, CSP, CPAE

Opportunity does not knock once, it knocks all the time. The trick is, we don't always recognize the sound. The key to becoming more successful is to **find opportunity in everyday life**—not just wait for that life-altering, retire-in-the-Caribbean bolt from the blue.

Here's how to start: **Each day this month, you're going to take a good, hard look at one aspect of your job, business, or presentation…and improve it.**

- Some people choose to think about their improvement goal first thing in the morning; others decide the night before. Either way works—but choose one and stick with it.
- In addition to considering what you want to change, you need to think about why you want to change it. How will it make your life or business better?
- Visualize, act, and carry yourself in the way that you aspire to be, not what you are.
- Write down your goal in a place where you'll see it several times a day, whether in a day planner, a sticky note on your computer, or clipped to your car dashboard.

The Chinese philosopher Lao-tzu famously said, "A journey of a thousand miles begins with a single step." **By making one small improvement every day, you will find in a very short period of time you'll be well on your way to becoming more successful than you ever thought possible.** When you see how well it works for a month, **you will want** to make it a lifelong habit—and as I like to remind people, "We choose our habits."

Patricia Fripp, CSP, CPAE

Patricia is virtually everywhere with www.FrippVT.com.

Fripp helps organizations and individuals gain a competitive edge through powerful persuasive presentation skills.

527 Hugo Street, San Francisco, CA 94122

(415)753-6556, Fax (415)753-0914

PFripp@ix.netcom.com, www.fripp.com

www.fripp.com/blog/ twitter@Pfripp

BOOK THREE: YOUR POWER TO MAKE MONEY

Power Time Management helps you make more money by focusing on essential skills, strategies and actions. In this section we'll cover these topics:

- Make Money
- Use a Double-Punch: *Your Secret Charisma* Plus *Power Time Management*
- Power of Focus-Point-Mastery (One Page Business Plan)

MAKE MONEY
(#1 of Make Money)

Want to use Power Time Management to help you make more money? What helps is to focus on high yield actions and implement them consistently. We'll use the M.O.N.E.Y. process:

M – make assets
O – open to new ideas and setup systems
N – nurture yourself
E – encourage relationships
Y – yearn for both more and enjoying this moment

1. Make assets
Focus on assets, not money. – Robert Kiyosaki

This quote may seem extreme. However, it does remind us that it helps to focus on creating sources of continuing income. Focusing only on working more hours for an hourly wage creates a real problem. This problem is that every person has a limit to how many productive hours he or she has in a week.

So let's go back to focusing on making assets. Some financial experts mention that most automobiles do NOT function as assets because they continually lose value the longer you own them.

So what is a real asset? Here are examples:
- rental property (you receive rental fees from residents every month
- your education
- a book (you receive residual income)
- a song
- a system which you can train others to provide

One of my favorite examples of such a system is:
Professional Coach and author C.J. Hayden teaches people how to get more clients. She also licenses Get Clients Now Facilitators. She notes, "Your first two clients will repay the cost of your license!"

Her program includes the following:

- Eleven hours of facilitator training
- Comprehensive Facilitator's Kit
- Unlimited renewable teaching license
- Ongoing support and community.

C.J.'s package (Facilitator training, Kit, and Teaching License) is $595.00. By the way, participants must renew their license each year for $99.00.

Additionally, C.J. states at her website: "Your facilitator's license requires that each person who participates in your programs must own a copy of the *Get Clients Now!* book." That's more book sales for C.J.

C.J. does not even teach the program. She has two people, "experienced business coaches personally selected by C.J.," provide the facilitator training.

C.J. can make only a limited amount of money by being in the room (or on the phone) and coaching one client at a time. Or the ceiling can be eliminated in that she can have numerous Facilitators all around the world. At this time, I see that her work is ongoing in 19 countries.

2. Open to new ideas and setup systems

One of the ways to effectively make more money is to use a system.

Do what you need to do to learn new ideas and systems. Study. Read. Attend an online seminar. Also, review what's working for you and then form your *own* system.

For example, several people have a system of buying a house, fixing it up and then selling it for a profit. Once they have such a system they repeat the process again and again.

My productivity soared when I devised a system for writing books. Here's my system that I first shared in my book *Love Yourself to Financial Abundance and Spiritual Joy*:

How You Can Take the Suffering Out of Writing

At this moment, I have 24 books on Amazon.com. Many of them are in both paperback and Amazon Kindle forms.

Writing can expand your financial abundance. One thing that is great about this work is: You write the book *one time* and it keeps bringing in money, month after month.

Many people start writing a book but soon quit. Why? The way they go about writing a book creates needless suffering.

Instead, here are *7 Methods to Take Suffering Out of Writing*. The essence of this process is *teamwork*.

1. Save Time and Aggravation by Using the process of "__MORE__"

When I do not have the perfect word or sentence, I simply write "__MORE__" and continue writing my first draft. My father is the opposite. Each sentence must be perfect before he writes the next sentence. One of my friends said, "Tom, that's why you've written 22 books, and he's written none."

I'm able to write at a good pace because I know that I'll revisit the material in my next pass at the project.

2. Read the First Draft Aloud to Someone

My next step is to read my first draft aloud to someone. I revise the material as I read it to the person. Using this method, I find so many errors and opportunities to refine the material.

3. Talk it through with a Developmental Editor

I hire an editor who goes through the material and writes notes for me within the actual paragraphs. She places her comments in between "[ ]". On occasion, she includes a comment like: "It would be good if you'd address the situation of ..."

This helps me. Besides I find it interesting to have a *dialogue* with my editor on paper.

4. Revise after the Developmental Editor's Notes

As I handle each detail the Development Editor brings up, I know the material is getting better.

5. Have a Copyeditor Go Through the Material, and Then You Personally Revise the Material

My copyeditor goes through the material line by line to find any punctuation errors or missing words.

Then, I revise the material again. Sometimes, I put things back because I have my own style; other times I don't. But it's nice to have those options to choose from.

6. Submit the Work to a Proofreader

I submit the work to a proofreader. A writer friend of mine mentioned that she views her own manuscript one final time because sometimes her proofreader misses an error or two.

7. Realize that the book is a *snapshot of what you felt and thought at that particular moment.*

Writers can paralyze themselves if they're trying to write "the definitive book." I write freely because I realize that every book is really just a snapshot of what I thought and felt at a particular time. Ultimately, I'll let my whole body of work stand for my thoughts. By the way, I hope to think deeper as I progress through life. So if I do not agree with what I wrote ten years ago, I'm okay with that. Further, I can write a revised edition at some point; my book *Be Heard and Be Trusted* is currently in its Third Edition.

As I mentioned above, I can summarize my *no-suffering method of writing* with one word: teamwork. Sometimes, I have three editors working on different parts of one book simultaneously. I find that having such momentum keeps up my morale. I also have to keep up with submitting material to three people. So the project progresses at a good pace.

3. Nurture yourself
Confidence attracts.
Lack of energy repels.

Optimism plus realism inspires.
Doom and gloom drains.

If you're feeling rundown with a decided lack of energy, it's easy to fall into the pattern of negative talking.

On the other hand, it's better to nurture your own energy level. Nurture yourself. The basics include: exercise, rest, and good nutrition.

Spiritual and mental "nutrition" are also vital. Some of my clients focus on:
- meditation
- spiritual retreat events
- reading spiritual materials
- prayer sessions

Recently, a number of researchers are noting the vital role that "play" has in the lives of highly-productive adults.

Play often includes activities that you find intrinsically valuable. Some people enjoy playing tennis with a friend. Others enjoy taking walks in nature.

I truly enjoy listening to music and assembling a jigsaw puzzle. It's a time in my day when I slow down and relax.

What activity would help you feel relaxed? What can you

do that would help you feel nurtured?

To earn money on a higher level and handle related stress, you need more energy. Be sure to nurture yourself.

4. Encourage relationships

I frequently share with clients and college students my phrase: "Use the 3 Magic Words of Networking: *Help Them First.*"

The good news is that you can help a person in some simple way. For example, I recently noted that an author I know was mentioned in someone's book. I contacted the author and alerted him to the mention. He ended up buying that particular book. Actually, the interaction ended up benefiting both authors.

Become known as a hub of influence (someone who connects people). I've received Facebook chat messages that have begun with: "Tom, since you know so many people, I was wondering if . . ."

Being a hub of influence can help you because people appreciate making new, valuable connections. I often ask, "Who is your ideal client?" and "How can I be supportive of what you're doing?" People often respond with a big smile because they appreciate the chance to talk about what they're doing and hope to gain more business.

To develop your relationships, take action so that you fulfill what I call the T.H.O.R. characteristics:

T – trustworthy
H – helpful
O – organized
R – respectful

The T.H.O.R. characteristics form a powerful, positive personal brand.

Your personal brand helps you make better connections faster. The personal brand relates to this question: "What are you best known for?"

People with a positive personal brand and great relationships succeed on a higher level.

5. Yearn for both "more" and "enjoying this moment"

By all reports and his own writing, Donald Trump likes making deals. So as he "goes for more" he is *also* enjoying the moment.

Find something that you're deeply interested in. Why? You'll put much more time and effort into the activity.

The size of your success is measured by the strength of your desire; the size of your dream; and how you handle disappointment along the way — Robert T. Kiyosaki

So enjoying the way you earn money can sustain you during the tough times.

Another important point is: Realize that this is an "AND-universe." By this I mean, you can enjoy the moment *and* still reach for more. I prefer to call it "different." *To reach for different.* Sometimes it's helpful to think of reaching for "more" as reaching for "different."

For example, your real enjoyment may not come from having "more" that is, seven vacations a year. It may arise from having *two* well-chosen vacations that you cherish.

I learned this detail powerfully several years ago. At one point, I was helping a team pull together speakers. I learned that bestselling author Richard Carlson was earning $20,000 a speech *but he put a limit* on the number of speaking engagements that he would accept each year.

This was a good choice on his part. He was able to devote

more time to his wife and two daughters. This meant a lot because he died at age 45. His wife and daughters have good memories of their times shared together.

Live your life every moment of every day, you never know what could happen. Your life is ticking away a minute at a time, enjoy it, live it, love it. – Julia Doherty

When you immerse yourself in daily life and you enjoy life, you become more attractive to people and opportunities.

So go for both: enjoy this moment and go for "different."

Ask yourself: "What different thing would I like to add to my life? It's an AND-universe and I'm grateful."

Principle
Making more money involves developing assets and nurturing your personal energy

Power Question
How will you study or look into making assets? What will you do today to nurture yourself so that you have the energy needed for making more money?

* * * * * *

USE A DOUBLE-PUNCH: *YOUR SECRET CHARISMA* PLUS *POWER TIME MANAGEMENT*
(#2 of Make Money)

Want to take your success and feelings of well-being to a higher level? My client "Athena" really wanted to make a breakthrough in her life. At first, she said that she just couldn't wrap her mind around the idea I just shared with her.

Just a moment earlier, I had shared with her, "I'm the only coach who combines *Your Secret Charisma* and *Power Time Management.*"

"I don't see how those two are connected," Athena protested.

Then I explained:

When I guide you to enhance charisma, you gain people's trust faster. Trust helps you save time.

I have another term for *Your Secret Charisma:* I also call it your *Warm Trust Charisma.* In any given moment, you can do something that creates trust between you and another person or, unfortunately, you could fall into some default-action that breaks trust down.

Now, we'll cover the T.I.M.E. process that relates to both charisma and power time management:

T – target listening
I – increase closeness
M – move ahead faster (teamwork)
E - encourage real health

1. Target listening
One of the best ways to create trust is: **Listen first.**

Many of us are desperate to be heard. (That's why I titled one of my books *Be Heard and Be Trusted.*)

Also, a significant number of people will sacrifice their personal happiness in order to feel "proven right."

Starting with these two details, you can help the other

person feel both heard and "right." How?

Listen to her.

One way to demonstrate that you're listening is to offer *Reflective Replies*. That is, reflect back the person's feelings.

Say things like:
- "That sounds frustrating"
- "That sounds disappointing."

It's important to say, "That sounds" so that you do NOT appear to be telling someone how he or she is feeling.

If you use Reflective Replies, you'll hear the person say something like this in response:
- "Yeah! It was frustrating! Let me tell what happened next."
- "It was intense. Then he started to . . ."

With the process of Reflective Replies, the other person knows that you're paying close attention. And she likes this!

2. Increase closeness

In any conversation, your comments can either create closeness and rapport or it can create the opposite: separation.

Here are two valuable methods.

a) Give affirmations related to the person.

Affirm something good about the person and his or her actions. Be specific.

Here are examples:
- "Your work on the budget was excellent. I could see it in the investor's face. She was convinced. I think your work really helped us close the deal."
- "Your work on the logo, especially adding the subtle smile, really warmed up the potential

clients. Three of them have said good things about the logo."

b) Say "I agree."

So many of us enter a conversation trying desperately to prove that we're right about something. It feels so good when our listeners confirm our rightness.

If possible, say "I agree" about some detail that the person offered. After you say, "I agree," the other person can breathe easier. Now he or she does *not* feel the need to prove a point.

Often, a positive side effect is that the person likes you!

3. Move ahead faster (teamwork)

Leadership is the art of getting someone else to do something you want done because he wants to do it. – Dwight D. Eisenhower

A great leader radiates Warm Trust Charisma. The leader demonstrates the 2 Cs: competence and compassion.

People don't care how much you know until they know how much you care. – John C. Maxwell

Show that you care by paying close attention to the team member as a person. The team member has personal reasons to do any action. Observe carefully. Ask some questions with a gentle tone.

Here are examples:
- "What about this project is interesting to you?"
- "How can doing this XZ report help your career?"

Later, you can remember what he or she finds personally

important and then interweave details about such personal benefits in your conversation.

Here's an example:

"Sarah, thanks for your work on the budget. I feel the investor will really key into the 1-2-3 section. By the way, now that you know about 1-2-3, you can use that when you achieve your next promotion."

In brief, you can **move ahead faster** in your own career when you support other people on the team—and they *know* that you're both competent and compassionate.

4. Encourage real health

To get more done (power time management), you need lots of energy.

It helps to have two forms of health: a) health in body and b) health in connecting (relationships)

Healthy communication builds you up.

On the other hand, unhealthy interactions can tear you down. For example, some time ago, one of my extended family members said really disparaging remarks to me on the phone. I could literally feel myself breaking down physically. My throat got worse, and my body aches increased.

Finally, I said, "Your criticism is making me feel bad. I do not have time for people who tear me down."

I ended the conversation. [*Later*, I had healthy interactions with this elderly person.]

My point is: **engage in healthy interactions and avoid or end unhealthy conversations.**

Lack of health steals your energy.

Further, it deflates your Warm Trust Charisma and cripples your productivity.

But this is NOT for you.
Remember to implement:

T – target listening
I – increase closeness
M – move ahead faster (teamwork)
E - encourage real health

Principle
Enhance your charisma, and you gain people's trust faster. Trust helps you save time.

Power Questions
How are you increasing people's trust in you? What can you add or delete from how you interact and thus improve your conversations?

* * * * * * *

POWER OF FOCUS-POINT-MASTERY (ONE PAGE BUSINESS PLAN)
(#3 of Make Money)

Would you like to get more done and feel better about your life? When you focus on what you really want and develop a focused-plan, you'll feel better because you'll have both marching orders and true clarity.

On the other hand, without a focus point, we scatter our energy. I've developed the One Page Business Plan that I carry with me every day.

The ultimate benefits of a One Page Business Plan are:

- more productivity
- time savings
- clarity
- focus on activities that generate personal good feelings and fulfillment
- focus on activities that generate profit

An old phrase is: "You get what you think about most." When you use a One Page Business Plan, you're thinking in a focused and positive manner.

Here are the topics that go on one 8.5 x 11 inch sheet of paper (suitable for a wallet or purse):

[See the next page.]

One Page Business Plan

- Mission:

- Top Goals with Due Dates:

- Ultimate Goals:

- Current Areas to Feel Good About and Feel Excited About (What works)

- Current Leadership-Growth Areas (includes keeping team members strong and happy)

- Current Areas to Measure

- Current Areas to Improve

- Current Areas to Watch Carefully (monitor and improve)

- [Your First Name,] What Are You Looking Forward to Experiencing and to Feeling?

- 3 Levels of Goals: Good, Better, Outrageous

- Effort Goals . . . Result Goals

- Other Notes:

© Tom Marcoux   Tom's Blog: BeHeardandBeTrusted.com

The *One Page Business Plan* is the center of *Focus-Point-Mastery*. The idea is to approach your daily life like you're a master of Power Time Management. It's really about you becoming skillful in making things happen that increase your joy and fulfillment.

Since there are 11 elements of the One Page Business Plan and I want to summarize the overall process, I'll now provide a few details per section.

1. Mission

It's best when your mission is beyond just making money. For example, my company's mission is: *We create energizing, encouraging edutainment for our good and humankind's rise.*

I include "our good" because strong and happy people make things turn out better for customers. Further, I make sure that team members fulfill some personal goals. It keeps them motivated to devote their best efforts.

2. Top Goals with Due Dates

Due dates are crucial; otherwise, things are too vague. Without due dates, productivity suffers.

3. Ultimate Goals

One of my ultimate goals is for my fantasy-thriller franchise *Jack AngelSword* to be so successful so that near the end of my lifespan Disney will want to buy my company. This would insure that millions of people would be served by my work beyond my lifetime. How fun!

4. Current Areas to Feel Good About and Feel Excited About (What works)

Never under estimate the power of good, empowering feelings to carry you forward through any tough times.

5. **Current Leadership-Growth Areas (includes keeping team members strong and happy)**

Every leader has weak areas and blind spots. It's good to identify details to work on. Good leaders develop loyal and productive teams.

6. **Current Areas to Measure**

I emphasize: *"Don't guess. Measure for success."* For example, I identified a target of writing 400 words a day which alerted me that I had 170 days to go on a certain project. A benefit of measuring your progress is that you raise your own morale!

7. **Current Areas to Improve**

People who are serious about increasing their joy and fulfillment monitor how they're currently doing. They also identify how they can get better at what they do.

8. **Current Areas to Watch Carefully (monitor and improve)**

In business, leaders are advised to pay attention to Key Performance Indicators and "critical measures." Two such measures can include number of sales meetings and closed sales. Which critical areas do you need to monitor and improve?

9. **[Your First Name,] What Are You Looking Forward to Experiencing and to Feeling?**

Imagine this: you can clearly see what all of your big efforts are going to bring to your life. Such clarity can motivate you on a daily basis. What do you really want? Research data shows that many people simply want to feel happy and secure. How will accomplishing your business goals bring you such feelings?

10. Three Levels of Goals: Good, Better, Outrageous

Some people set goals that are too extreme. Others set goals that are too low and un-motivating.

I've learned that it's better to set three levels for goals: Good, Better, Outrageous. Another way to say it is "Outrageous Good Results."

Here's an example:

One author I know sells 25 books each month. She can set a "Better" goal of 300 books. Then, for "Outrageous" she can set 4,000 books sold per month. To reach for the 4,000 level, her thinking must expand. Now, she's thinking of ideas like: "How can I team up with other authors so that we can promote our respective books to each other's e-lists?"

Three levels of goals gives you the space to think bigger and allow the universe to give you "happy surprises."

11. Effort Goals . . . Result Goals

In sales, an Effort Goal can be "make 30 marketing calls this week." A related Result Goal might be "gain three new clients." We notice: You can't get a Result Goal without taking action on an Effort Goal.

You can be proud of yourself for your actions on Effort Goals regardless of whether you meet a Result Goal this week or next month. The truth is: Result Goals are often based on things out of our control. The good news is that we can control our personal efforts toward Effort Goals.

* * *

Here is the essence of the One Page Business Plan:
We are motivated by what we want to feel.

We generally change ourselves for one of two reasons: inspiration or desperation. — Jim Rohn

Another way to look at this is:
What do you want to feel?
And what do you want to STOP feeling?

Many people are wired in such a way that they'll do more to end some form of pain than make the efforts for something vaguely positive.

The One Page Business Plan helps you identify your clear, focused plan of action.

I've noticed that many people will put more effort into planning a vacation than planning their life.

But this is NOT for you.

Use a One Page Business Plan that's focused on business-related goals, and you're likely to expand your success. More success may lead to more vacations!

Principle
Using a One Page Business Plan helps you focus on critical factors to improve both your business efforts AND your feelings of fulfillment.

Power Question
What would you put into the categories of your One Page Business Plan?

* * *

Now, that we're talking about planning, we'll explore business insights provided by Ed Gandia.

Massive Action: The Unspoken Ingredient of Freelance Success
by Ed Gandia

Summary: Freelance success can be hard and it means prospecting all the time. But by committing to taking serious, focused and MASSIVE action, you're virtually guaranteed success.

If I had to name just ONE reason why so many solo professionals fail to achieve their goals it would be this:

Failure to take MASSIVE action on a continual basis.

Action alone will usually move you in the direction of your goals. But it's not guaranteed. However, if you commit to taking serious, focused and MASSIVE action, you're virtually guaranteed success.

That's an idea I implemented early in my freelance career, and it's a big reason why I was able to quit my day job to go solo after moonlighting as a freelancer for just 27 months.

I created a list of what I *thought* I needed to do to achieve that goal... and then I DOUBLED it. By doubling the amount of action I thought I'd need to take, I virtually assured that I'd achieve my dream of a freelance career.

If you study successful people in any field, you find the same pattern. Those who overcome what seem to be insurmountable challenges do so because they took massive action. And they kept at it, day after day.

Where Do You Start?

But where (and when!) do you start? What do you do

first? And second? How do you establish priorities? How can you break this monolith task (of landing work now!) into attainable chunks?

If you want to get out of your current situation as soon as possible, the trick is to get started right away. Don't wait. Take action while your excitement is high and you're motivated to take those first few steps.

What follows is a simple framework (and a bit of inspiration) for taking massive action on a weekly basis.

Take Quick Action

Let's start by quickly assessing where you are. How are you feeling? Is this all a bit overwhelming? Are you feeling anxious or confused? Are you really desperate to get work in the door and pay some bills?

If so, then this is how you should start:
- Pick **one** prospecting strategy
- Write down **three** simple and quick steps you can take in the next three days to implement that strategy
- Then do it!

Pick something you can do **immediately**, something you can do **tomorrow**, and something you can do **the day after**.

Pick tasks that shouldn't take you long to accomplish. They should also be tasks that will give you quick wins, even if they're small, psychological victories.

For instance, if your strategy is to creatively approach a few past clients, then maybe your first task is to make a list of the five or six clients you want to contact. On day two maybe you detail the approach you're going to take for each client, based on the ideas from Strategy #1. And on day three, you contact all six of them via email and phone.

Frankly, it doesn't really matter what three tasks you pick

for this exercise, as long as they help you implement at least one of the strategies—**and as long as you commit to doing them as if your life depended on their accomplishment.**

Don't underestimate the effect these baby steps will have on your psyche. Sure, this may not be considered "massive" action. But if you feel overwhelmed, taking even the smallest action will get you on the right path and will start building the momentum you need to keep yourself focused.

Get a Quick Win

Closely related to taking quick action is getting a quick win. Even though your longer-term goal may be to get out of this "I need work NOW!" situation on a more permanent basis, a more pressing goal is to land one gig—any paying gig—as soon as possible. And to go about pursuing this goal with confident expectations and a sense of joy and purpose.

The gig doesn't have to be great. It doesn't have to be the one that pays all the bills. **It just has to be enough to prove to you that you're moving in the right direction!**

A quick win will provide the fuel you need to get back on the superhighway of success—and the protection you need to avert negative downward spirals.

Sometimes our bigger goals overwhelm us when we're struggling badly. But small, quick wins seem much more attainable. And when you land it, the impact it can have on your self-confidence and drive can be just as big as landing that huge client.

So go easy on yourself. Yes, we're going to set some big goals, but if you're feeling overwhelmed and dejected, set yourself up for some quick wins too. They can make ALL the difference in getting back on track. And your quick action steps will help get you there.

Determine the Size and Nature of the Gap

Okay, so once you've taken some quick action and have landed (or are working on landing) some quick wins, now's the time to take a step back and analyze the current state of your freelance business.

How much work do you need—now and longer term? Do you need to land more gigs right away or do you have some breathing space? What would it take to get you to a manageable state?

If the gap between where you are now and where you need (or want) to be is huge, don't be discouraged. Draw motivation and power from the fact that you and the Universe are in control of bridging that gap.

Not some bureaucrat, not some "exploratory committee."

Yes, you have work to do. But take comfort in knowing that the tools and strategies you need to narrow that gap are things you already know about and have done in the past. They do NOT involve some sort of "ninja" marketing technique.

Draft a Simple Action Plan

Once you've reviewed your current situation and you have a sense of what it would take to bridge the gap between where you are and where you'd like to be, draft a simple action plan based on what you've learned so far.

It doesn't have to be fancy. All you need is a straightforward list of strategies with clear action steps under each idea. List a date next to each action item indicating when you'll start that effort.

Again, don't try to do it all. Pick the strategies that resonate best with you and are a good fit for your specific situation. From there, prioritize your strategies based on their likelihood to yield results fast.

How do you know what will work best? Think about how you landed your last 10 clients? What specific marketing strategy or effort helped you land each of them? List them out one by one. And start with the strategies that enabled you to land the most clients.

In other words, when in doubt, stick to what's already been working for you.

Also, remember to limit the number of strategies you implement. I typically advise freelancers to have no more than two to four marketing strategies in play at any given time. However, **if you're looking for work NOW, it's okay to expand that number to maybe three to six strategies.**

But that's about the upper limit if you want to keep your sanity. It's just too hard to do any of them well if you're spread too thin. So choose wisely.

Your basic action plan could look something like this:
- Day 1: Draft list of 6+ current and former clients and contact all 6.
- Day 2: Go through my hard drive and email archives and find all projects quoted over the last 2 years.
- Day 3: Email/call at least 5 prospects to whom I quoted work in the last 2 yrs.
- Day 4: Draft a simple script for friends/relatives that explains what I do in layman's terms. Also, contact 10 friends, relatives and colleagues to see if they can refer me to someone.
- Day 5: Spend all morning searching through LinkedIn groups to see if I find meaningful connections I could leverage in warm emails to select prospects.

You get the point. The idea is to commit to key actions every day. As the week progresses, you may have to adjust your plan. You may have to spend more time on one activity than you had previously expected.

Or maybe suddenly you'll land a project! That's fine. Just keep moving along so you don't lose your momentum. And if you DO land a project, don't stop prospecting! Keep at it, even if it means scaling down your effort to just three or four hours a week.

Focus on Action, Not Outcome

As you develop your action plan, I encourage you to **focus your goals, attention and energy on action, not outcome.** For example, it's better to have a goal of sending 15 emails to previous clients and prospects and contacting 10 people in your professional network than to have a goal of landing a new client.

This may go against much of the success literature out there. But I've found that although you can't control when you'll achieve your ultimate goal, you can control what you'll do to reach that goal.

Think "Ready, Fire, Aim"

Also, don't get caught up in getting everything perfect before you put it into action. According to Michael Masterson, author of the bestselling book *Ready, Fire, Aim: Zero to $100 Million in No Time Flat* (Wiley, 2008), most people spend too much time trying to get things just right before they take action. In other words, they practice a "ready, aim, fire" philosophy.

Masterson says, "The nothing-less-than-perfect attitude has been the theme of many success stories, but it is exactly the wrong notion to have in your head when it's time to launch a new product or business. When the time is right, you must fire. If you spend another moment aiming, the opportunity to hit your target may pass you by."

So don't wait until everything's perfect before implementing these ideas. It doesn't really matter where you start. Just start... now!

Don't Put Goals on a Pedestal

At the same time, don't limit the goals you put in your action plan because you think they might be too "grand." None of them deserve to be put on a pedestal. I realize that when you're in a tight situation, goals that may have seemed completely doable before now seem larger than life.

But that's just your current perception. It's not reality. I know this from experience. Every worthwhile goal I've reached became far easier to attain when I stopped worrying about the goal's "grandness."

For instance, when I was in sales, I started landing large sales only after I downplayed the difficulty and skill needed to land them. I also quit my day job only after I stopped being scared and realized that quitting my job was just the last step in a well-executed plan.

Same thing happened when I decided to start writing white papers for clients. I had never written one before, and the thought of charging $3,000-$6,000 for this service was terrifying!

But I went for it anyway. And eventually I landed my first white paper project. Which led to another, and then another and so on.

Today, I don't give it a second thought. I regularly charge $5,000-$6,000 for these pieces and land most of the ones I quote.

Remember: It's Your Full-Time Job!

Finally, if you have zero (or little) work right now, accept the fact that your full-time job is to find work. That means you need to spend 95% (or more) of your working hours actively looking for opportunities.

Naturally, once you land a project or two, you can scale back your search. But until you do, it's full steam ahead!

When finding work is your full-time job, you need to treat it as such. Schedule every hour. Know what you'll be working on and when. And be very clear about your daily action objectives are.

Be aggressive but also realistic about how much you can accomplish in a given day. And give yourself permission to work on these strategies all day long until you start landing work.

Be Tenacious

Just as important as setting actionable objectives and taking massive action is your state of mind while you do it. One of the biggest reasons freelancers fail to get out of a rut is that they give up too soon. They get discouraged at the first sign of rejection and decide that maybe they were meant to struggle.

After all, we're in a tough economy, right?

Nothing could be further from the truth. As a business of one, you don't have to bring in truckloads of business just to keep the lights on (as opposed to most traditional brick-and-mortar businesses that need tons of work just to meet their monthly payroll!)

Just ONE decent gig can give you the breathing room you need to get back on track financially and emotionally. You can then build on that foundation and climb out of that hole.

Will it be hard? You bet! Can you do it? I have no doubt. But your strength and resolve will be tested. And when that happens, remember this:

It's always darkest and coldest right before dawn!

Try to Relax!
The idea is to go about your plan with a sense of urgency...but also with confident expectations. Set your goals. Draft your plan. Start taking action.

And then just "let go" and let the Universe do its thing.

Let the Magic Happen
Have you ever watched *The Lord of the Rings* trilogy? If not, I highly recommend it. This classic story is a powerful reminder that amazing things happen when we move confidently in the direction of our dreams. In fact, the movie can be summarized in these words from Dorothea Brande:

Act boldly and unseen forces will come to your aid.

I know that may sound a bit woo-woo. But I know it to be true in my heart. Over and over again, when I've acted boldly, with confidence and a great sense of calm, things have happened that I just can't explain.

It will go something like this: soon after you begin to implement these ideas, you'll get a call from an old client—someone you hadn't yet even contacted and maybe even forgot you had done business with years ago.

Or some random prospect will email you because he found you through a Google search.

The details don't matter. What does matter is that this prospect (or prospects!) will come to you out of the blue. And one or more of them will turn into clients. In fact, they may very well solve your immediate problem!

At first, you'll be grateful for the unexpected win. And you may even think to yourself, "Wow, that was cool. I landed some work before the ideas from this episode could take their course."

That may very well be true. But I submit to you that these serendipitous events (new clients suddenly calling you to give you work) will be the result of your new commitment to find and land work fast.

In other words, it was your faith and your resolve that somehow attracted these good things your way. This training episode was simply the spark that ignited your confidence and got you moving in the right direction.

So if this happens (and it WILL happen to some of you), honor and welcome this blind "luck" for what it really is: your renewed faith in yourself and what you can accomplish.

So, yes, take massive action. Go at it like a true champ. But know that you're not alone.

The Universe rewards confident action. In a BIG way!

Ed Gandia teaches freelancers how to create a business that enables them to earn more in less time, doing work they love, for better clients. He's the co-author of the bestselling and award-winning book *The Wealthy Freelancer*, founder of International Freelancers Academy
www.internationalfreelancersacademy.com
and host of The High-Income Business Writing podcast www.b2blauncher.com.

* * *

Ed encouraged us to take massive action. Now, Chip Conley invites us to focus our actions in ways that put service in the forefront and attract massive profit—and feelings of fulfillment.

The 7 Practices of Peak Leadership
by Chip Conley

Why don't we "practice" business? I've come to realize that—unlike medicine and law—we don't think of our profession as business leaders as a "practice." A few years ago, in the last downturn, I developed the principles of PEAK as an alternative operating model for my business based upon Abraham Maslow's iconic Hierarchy of Needs pyramid. Reinterpreting this well-known theory of human motivation helped me to see that all stakeholders associated with a company have their own Hierarchy of Needs. My company Joie de Vivre tripled in size during this difficult period and I came to find out that a variety of other transformational companies like Harley-Davidson have used Maslow's theory as a foundation for their business model.

Business principles are only as good as the practices that back them up. Recently, with the assistance of some good friends, I've developed a set of PEAK Leadership practices that can assist any leader or leadership team to move from survival to success and on to being a transformative role model in their industry. When a company embeds these principles and practices in how they grow their leaders, the end result is PEAK performance: a phenomenon of sustained growth—both for the organization as well as for those within the organization.

Practice 1: Embody an inherently positive view of human nature.

The principles of PEAK have their roots in humanistic psychology and a basic belief that man is meant to "be all that he can be." So, it's not surprising that the fundamental first practice is assuring that a PEAK leader believes that humans—at their very core—gravitate to goodness when the right conditions exist for them to flourish.

Creating what Maslow called "psycho-hygiene" in a company means focusing on people's best qualities and believing in what's been known for a half-century in business as a "Theory Y" perspective on management versus "Theory X." With Theory X, management assumes employees are inherently lazy and will avoid work if they can. As a result of this, management believes that workers need to be closely supervised and a comprehensive system of controls developed. With Theory Y, management assumes employees may be ambitious and self-motivated. They believe the satisfaction of doing a good job is a strong motivation and seek to create the conditions for the employee to develop their own strengths to be successful. While this latter theory may feel intuitively right to many of us, is your organization still structured in a Theory X style of business?

Practice 2: Create the conditions for people to live their callings.

Great leaders understand there are only three relationships you can have with your work: a job, a career, or a calling. A job tends to deplete you and a calling energizes you. Most employees live in the bartering world of work. The company gives them a compensation package and recognition and, in return, the employee gives their time and energy. Yet, those that are living their calling have moved from external to internal motivation. And, these employees are not exclusively focused on the specific collection of tasks they perform and are more focused on the impact or purpose of what they do. The best hospitals have more nurses living their calling. The best airlines have the happiest flight attendants (Southwest). What are you doing to help your people find their sense of calling in what they do?

Practice 3: Promote and measure the value of intangibles.

In business, we are taught that leadership is all about managing what you can measure, but what's most easily measurable is the tangible in life. Yet, is it the tangible or the intangible in business and life that creates value? In business, the metrics that track the tangible are well known: your profitability, assets & liabilities, cost structure, market share. Yet, in reality, these tangible metrics are the result of a series of intangibles that drive excellence: brand loyalty and reputation, employee engagement, customer evangelism, the ability to innovate. Great leaders nurture, value, and evolve corporate culture—one of the most valuable intangibles—as a key differentiator for their company. These intangibles are the inputs that drive the tangible output that most companies use to evaluate their performance. In the 21st century, great leaders are learning how to measure and benchmark these intangibles so that they're not out of sight, out of mind. Which intangibles are most valuable to your business and how are you measuring them?

Practice 4: Ability to move fluidly between being a "transactional" and a "transformational leader."

Author James McGregor Burns once wrote that, "Transformational leaders look for the personal motives in followers, seek to satisfy higher needs, and engage the full person of the follower." Yet, most management decisions require only transactional thinking because the goal is purely to optimize existing resources. A great leader is able to move fluidly between addressing the foundational needs that people have, but also helping them see beyond the short-term so that they can be motivated by a compelling vision that helps them transcend their momentary challenges. How much of your time is stuck in the trenches as a transactional leader versus focusing on how to create transformation?

Practice 5: Calibrate the balance between "Conscious" and "Capitalism."

Business has quite often been seen as a "zero-sum" game. One person's win is another person's loss. Taken to the global level, some believe that capitalism's short-term gains are often to the long-term detriment of the environment and to certain communities. And, at this crossroads, in an increasingly transparent world, this is why great leaders have to think more broadly about the impact of their decisions, not just on the bottom line, but on their broader stakeholders. In many ways, Wal-Mart took this step when they saw their stock price flat line even with sizable revenue and net income growth. Yet, for those socially conscious business leaders, cash flow is the blood that keeps your organization alive. Make sure the basic survival needs of your company are met. How do you balance the priorities of the broader community versus the financial needs of your company?

Practice 6: Focus on your customers' highest needs.

Henry Ford once suggested, "If I asked my customers what they wanted, they would have said a faster horse." PEAK leaders and companies understand what the customer wants even before the customer has articulated it and they realize that customer innovation requires a certain amount of mind reading and cultural anthropology. By doing this well (with Apple being the best example in the world), you create a movement and evangelists and reduce your need to spend money on traditional marketing. Are your customer satisfaction surveys just asking the obvious questions that will track their expectations and desires, but not their unrecognized needs? How can you "mind read" your customers?

Practice 7: Lead to PEAK

Just as a Sherpa does in the Himalayas, great leaders meet their people where they are on the pyramid and help them to see the natural path to the peak. They recognize the value of loyalty and mentoring as a means of sustainable success in business. PEAK leaders champion personal development in tandem with corporate development knowing that there's a synergistic effect of having a self-actualized individual in the workplace as evidenced at companies like Google. And, most importantly, they embody authentic leadership by being, not just by doing. How are you incubating a collection of great leaders?

Conscious people pay attention. It's true of spiritual leaders. It's true of business leaders. PEAK leaders pay attention to the higher needs while not neglecting the base needs that provide a foundation for their organization. Leadership is all about making conscious choices and knowing that the higher you are in a company, the more magnified your decisions and behavior will be throughout the organization.

CHIP CONLEY
Hotel guru. Armchair psychologist. Traveling

philosopher. Author. Speaker. Teacher. Student.

Chip Conley has lived out more than one calling in his lifetime.

Founder and former CEO of Joie de Vivre (JDV), Chip has led the development, creation, and management of more boutique hotels than anyone else in the world. Starting JDV at age 26, his mission was to "create joy" by building a company that *USA Today* called "the most delightfully schizophrenic collection of hotels in America." During his 24 years as CEO, JDV grew to become the second largest boutique hotel company in America.

Chip shares his unique prescription for success in *PEAK: How Great Companies Get Their Mojo from Maslow*, based on noted psychologist Abraham Maslow's iconic Hierarchy of Needs. The New York Times bestseller, *EMOTIONAL EQUATIONS: Simple Truths for Creating Happiness + Success*, is Chip's latest book where he takes us from emotional intelligence to emotional fluency—placing meaning at the top of the balance sheet. His previous books include *The Rebel Rules: Daring to be Yourself in Business*, and *Marketing That Matters: 10 Practices to Profit Your Business and Change the World*. Chip presents his theories on transformation and meaning—in business and life—to audiences around the world and he's been a featured speaker at TED.

Honored with the 2012 Pioneer Award—hospitality's highest accolade—*The San Francisco Business Times* named Chip the Most Innovative CEO—and JDV the 2 in the entire Bay Area. Chip received his BA and MBA from Stanford University and holds an Honorary Doctorate in Psychology from Saybrook University, where he is the 2012/2013 ScholarPractitioner in residence. He served on the Glide Memorial Board for nearly a decade and is now on the Boards of the Burning Man Project, the Esalen Institute, and

Youth Speaks.

Chip's latest calling is traveling the globe—speaking about transformative business practices and seeking out the world's best festivals. He's on a mission to cultivate more cultural curiosity by sharing the "collective effervescence" found in the festival experience. Chip's travel blog is at FEST300.com and he is also AFAR magazine's festival correspondent at AFAR.com.

www.chipconley.com

BOOK FOUR:
YOUR POWER TO SAVE TIME AND GET THE BEST FROM PEOPLE

Power Time Management helps you save time by using great relationship-building skills. In this section we'll cover these topics:

- Power of Your Principles
- Make It Easy for People to Say "Yes" to You

POWER OF YOUR PRINCIPLES
(#1 of Save Time and Get the Best from People)

To do the right things sooner and to save time, it helps to identify your principles. You can look at a principle as a tool to help you have "pre-made decisions."

When people see that you operate with principles, they trust you faster. Why? You are consistent.

For example, one of my clients has this principle: "With

cranky, elderly family members, I do *not* return negativity for negativity." This makes her life easier. She knows that if she's feeling tired she will avoid visiting a cranky relative. The reason: She wants to live up to her principle of "not returning negativity for negativity."

I guide my clients to develop their principles so that they can prepare their Autopilot Coach. In essence, your Autopilot Coach is a positive voice in your head that guides you to make the right decisions in an efficient manner.

For example, I have programmed my own Autopilot Coach with these principles:
- Better than zero
- Worst first
- If in doubt, leave it out.
- Life is about success, not perfection.
- Don't guess. Measure it for success.

Here are examples from author/blogger Gretchen Rubin:
- Be Gretchen. [The first of her personal Twelve Commandments.]
- Act the way I want to feel. [Another one of her personal commandments]
- Happiness doesn't always make you feel happy [One of Gretchen's "Secrets of Adulthood."]

One thing you notice about the above listed principles is that they are concise ways of representing rather involved, profound ideas.

For example, my phrase "Better than zero" reminds me to do some small action every day because these actions will add up to big changes. For example, I write every day (sometimes only two paragraphs), and that has led to 361 pages that formed my collection of fiction entitled *TimePulse:*

Beyond Titanic.

Another example: Gretchen's principle "Be Gretchen" reminds her to honor the unique combination of virtues, needs, and quirkiness that are her makeup. She avoids trying to live up to being similar to anyone else.

Still another example: Gretchen's principle "Happiness doesn't always make you feel happy" reminds her that some actions may feel uncomfortable in the moment but they contribute to a feeling of real fulfillment.

Finally, here's a principle that I always remember:

Decision-making is easy when your values are clear.
– Roy O. Disney (Walt Disney's brother and business partner)

Walt Disney and his brother were offered many kinds of business opportunities, but they quickly dismissed those activities that were *not* aligned with "family entertainment."

Again, you can use your principles to streamline your process to make the decisions that work best for you.

Principle
Identify your principles and streamline your decision-making process.

Power Questions
What are the principles that you most want to use as your guidelines for life and business?

* * * * * *

MAKE IT EASY TO SAY "YES" TO YOU
(#2 of Save Time and Get the Best from People)

What's one way to get farther faster? Getting "yes" from people. It's best to make it easy to say "yes" to you. Toward that end, we'll use the E.A.S.Y. process:

E – encourage one simple action
A – arrange for you to do the "grunt work"
S – set forth a "first draft"
Y – yield to their timeframe

1. Encourage one simple action

I've noticed that people often make it tough to say "yes." Why? They ask for something too soon or they ask for too many things. Start small. What you want is to have an interaction in which the other person is engaged. When you give the other person something, they do not have to engage.

On the other hand, when you invite the person to do something simple for you, their brain actually shifts in perception. It's almost like their brain says, "Oh, I did something for Sam here. I guess I care."

Ask someone to pass the salad at dinner, and this interaction guides the other person to engage with you.

When you want someone to say "yes," to you, be sure to start with a small request.

2. Arrange for you to do the "grunt work"

A primary way to make it easy for someone to say "yes" is for you to do the difficult part of the project. For example, you'll see that two of the articles in this book are lightly edited transcripts of video messages by best-selling authors.

My team did the grunt work of transcribing the videos. The only thing the authors had to do was say "Yes, you can include the transcript in your 24th book, Tom."

That worked out well, and it went quickly.

3. Set forth a "first draft"

Just before my father completed his military service, he wrote drafts of recommendation letters. Then, he took these drafted letters to his commanding officers, who read the letters and simply signed them. They evidently agreed with my father's self-assessment. That was easy!

4. Yield to their timeframe

Some top people in business take a couple of weeks before they respond. When I work with them, I make sure to give them plenty of lead time. I do *not* want to be frantically waiting for them. I yield to *their* timeframe.

Here's an important detail: **No one likes to be pushed.** If you push for a fast response, the person may balk and simply do the easiest thing and say something like: "Thanks for asking me. I must say 'no' at this time. My schedule is too full."

Instead, give the person plenty of lead time. And then periodically check in with the person.

* * *

The person who moves forward faster in life is a master of working with people and gaining their cooperation. Practice the methods of the E.A.S.Y. process. And *before* you ask for anything, find a way to help that person. I refer to this sequence with the *3 Magic Words of Networking:* **Help Them First.**

Principle
You get more people saying "yes" when you make it easy for them.

Power Questions
How can you make your request seem like a small one? How can you take any inconvenience out of the process for the other person?

* * *

On the topic of making it easy for people to say "yes" to you, we'll now learn Mark Sanborn's insights about getting people to follow your lead.

8 Reasons Why People Won't Follow You
by Mark Sanborn

There's a familiar saying that if nobody is following you, you're just out taking a stroll. The question for leaders "out taking a stroll" is why nobody is following them?

If you're a leader and people aren't following you, consider the possible reasons:

1. They don't like you.
Research shows we'd rather work with incompetent people who are nice than competent people who aren't. If you treat people poorly and are generally unlikable, it is unlikely anybody will follow you unless they are scared to death to do otherwise. The notable exception in business history have been those unlikable leaders who had such visionary products that others were willing to put up with

their behavior. The question remains, however: how much more successful had these high fliers been if they'd paid more attention to likability?

2. They don't trust you.

I have a friend who is a blast to drink beer with. He's always got funny stories and the latest dirt to share. He discloses lots of things about others. And while I "like" him, I don't trust him. I know that when he's drinking beer with someone else, I'm likely to be the topic of his talking out of school.

I think trust is even more important than likability. While I may not like someone in a business situation, I can still do business with them without fear of being unjustly harmed or cheated.

3. They don't want to go where you're leading.

People are unwilling to go anywhere that doesn't represent a positive change. They can even handle the challenges and sacrifices of a new undertaking if they believe there is a payoff on arrival.

One client had a vision statement that was heavy on financial metrics but said nothing about the quality of life for employees or customers. I wasn't surprised that nobody could remember what the vision was, nor care about achieving it. Their vision statement became effective when it was rewritten to express the future for all stakeholders, including employees.

4. They don't know why they should do what you ask.

Kim is a young leader who is very focused and task-oriented. She is well known for issuing edicts and delegating tasks without explanation. She believes it makes her more time effective, and if anyone asks why, she calmly replied, "Because I said so."

"Because I said so" is tough for kids to swallow and more difficult for adults. Knowing why a request is made is something any intelligent adult would desire. Harried, leaders, however are often better at giving commands than explaining them or providing context.

5. They don't think you have their best interests at heart.

There are times you may ask an employee to do something simply because it is a condition of their job. Don't, however, think that subterfuge, spin or trickery is fair play. It will undermine your credibility. Be honest in the direct payoff–or lack thereof.

If you accomplish organizational goals at the expense of your team members, your legacy is that of tyrant. As overused as the phrase win/win may be, it is still a guiding principle of leaders who get followed.

6. The don't feel supported and/or appreciated.

Just because you pay people to work with you doesn't mean they don't deserve appreciation. A sincere thank you goes a long way towards a motivated team. And support means you care enough to remove barriers and provide the resources your team needs to win.

7. They don't have the training necessary to be good followers.

Phil is a beloved leader. When he picks someone to lead an important project, his initial conversation always includes this question: "Is there anything you'll need to learn now to be successful?"

No amount of motivation will help an employee succeed

if he or she doesn't posses the necessary skills. It you are leading a technology initiative, begin by identifying the skills it will take for employees to support you in the change.

8. They don't respect you.

People respect you for who you are, your competence and abilities, and your relationships with others. Who a follower chooses to follow and why tells much about him or her. That's why people are reluctant to follow others lacking integrity, ability or people skills. By giving allegiance to someone you don't respect, you loose a little self-respect in the process.

Nobody is perfect all the time, but those who get followed devote more time and effort to being the kind of leader who deserves to get followed.

Mark Sanborn is the president of Sanborn & Associates, Inc., an idea lab for leadership development.

In addition to his experience leading at a local and national level, he has written or co-authored 8 books and is the author of more than two dozen videos and audio training programs on leadership, change, teamwork and customer service. He has presented over 2400 speeches and seminars in every state and a dozen countries.

Mark is a member of the prestigious Speakers Roundtable, 20 of the top speakers in the world today. Mark holds the Certified Speaking Professional (CSP) from the National Speakers Association and is a member of the Speaker Hall of Fame (CPAE).

The author of 8 books, Mark's book, *The Fred Factor: How Passion in Your Work and Life Can Turn the Ordinary Into the Extraordinary* was an international bestseller and has sold over 2 million copies. The sequel, *Fred. 2.0*, was released in

March of 2013.

He is the leading authority on turning ordinary into extraordinary and is in demand as a speaker, author and advisor to leaders.

Contact Mark at www.MarkSanborn.com

* * *

Continuing our discussion about making it easy for people to say "yes" to you, we learn Rebecca Morgan's insights about how we treat our friends. Several reports note that many people gain jobs through connections made by friends. First, we need our friends to trust us.

Your Behavior with Friends May Influence Your Career
by Rebecca Morgan, CSP, CMC

We usually give our friends some slack, letting them slide when if they were a co-worker we might not.

But how about friends who we could refer for a job or consulting project? Do you let them get by with being irresponsible or self-absorbed?

I'm in the position to refer a lot of my collegial friends to possible new business. But—rightly or wrongly—I notice how they behave toward me as a determinant of if I want to put my reputation on the line by referring them.

A man who is also a consultant and trainer became a personal friend. When he had engagements in my area, I invited him to save the hour drive from his home and stay in my guest room. He often took me up on it. I enjoyed his company.

However, he rarely brought anything if he also came to dinner. In fact, he would sometimes say, "Do you have any wine?" as he entered empty handed.

He was also lax about returning my calls, even if I said it was to discuss a potential referral for him. Then when I did refer him, he let a week or so lapse before calling my connection who was expecting his call.

The last straw came when I invited him to a small dinner party. He knew only 5 others were attending. When he asked, "What can I bring that doesn't take cooking?" I nearly fainted, but I said, "No one else is bringing wine. Can you do that?" He said yes.

On the evening of the event all the other guests arrived. When he hadn't at 30 minutes past the designated arrival time, I got worried as I thought something must have happened to him. I called his cell phone—no answer so I left a voice mail. I also texted asking his estimated time of arrival. Nothing.

Another half hour passed and we sat down to dinner—wineless. I called and texted again. No response.

I figured something horrible happened. The next day, still nothing from him. The next week a mutual friend said she'd talked to him. I asked if he'd mentioned anything bad happening recently and she said no.

A few weeks later he called and left a message. I was relieved nothing horrible happened, but livid that he hadn't 1) bothered to call if he knew he couldn't make it so I could have provided the wine he'd promised, and 2) didn't respond to my calls expressing my concern for him.

While I enjoyed this man's company, he crossed the line. I'd given him slack in the past many times, but I could no longer tolerate his self-absorption, not only from a friend standpoint, but professionally. I could not in good conscience refer him again because of his irresponsible behavior. I couldn't be sure his bad judgment wouldn't also pay out in a client situation.

How do you behave toward your collegial friends? They may be determining if your behavior illustrates someone who's responsible, ethical and reliable. Or not.

Rebecca L. Morgan, CSP, CMC, specializes in creating innovative solutions for customer service challenges. She's appeared on 60 Minutes, Oprah, the *Wall Street Journal*, National Public Radio and *USA Today*. Rebecca is the bestselling author of 25 books, including *Calming Upset Customers* and *Professional Selling*. She is an exemplary resource who partners with you to accomplish high ROI on your strategic customer service projects. For information on her services, books, and resources, or for permission to repost or reprint this article, contact her at 408/998-7977, Rebecca@RebeccaMorgan.com, http://www.RebeccaMorgan.com/

* * * * * * *

This section is about saving time and getting the best from people. Both valuable goals begin with you and your own clarity of mind. Now, I'll share a powerful method from Jean Moroney.

How the 3-Minute Rule Can Save You Hours of Wasted Effort
by Jean Moroney

When you're under a deadline, or just plain busy, the last

thing you can afford is to bog down and waste time going in circles. That's why, if you've spent even one minute in indecision, puzzlement, or conflict, I recommend you stop what you're doing and take three minutes to "think on paper" to make sure you use your time well.

Bogging down is evidence you've overloaded your mental circuits. You may be having an argument in your mind: Should you work on the problem your boss just plopped in front of you, or the A-1 project due next week? Or you may be unclear on your current priority: Can the little stuff be put off one more day, or will that create a crisis this afternoon? Or maybe you're just confused about your next step: You know you need to put together a report, but what exactly should go in it? There are lots of possibilities.

When you're overloaded, you can't think straight, so you don't make good decisions. But right then, in the trenches, you need a good decision about how to spend your time now.

In such a situation, I recommend using the #1 tactic to put your mind in gear, "thinking on paper." "Thinking on paper" is what it sounds like—it's writing out your thoughts in full sentences as you think them. When your thoughts are tangled in your head, getting them out onto paper helps you untangle them. "Thinking on paper" helps you root out problems, make good judgments and get creative. It gives you the extra mental leverage you need when you're overloaded.

Here's how to do it:

Start with a goal. Write down the question you need to answer at the top of the page. Perhaps it's "What should I be doing?" or "What's the problem here?" Just the discipline of writing out your goal sets your purpose in your mind, zeros you in on the most important issues, and helps you think step-by-step.

Then start acting like a court reporter, transcribing the words in your mind into full sentences. Capturing the full sentences is the key to the process. Often when you think in your head, the thoughts flit by as a word or a phrase. When you slow down and express them in full sentences, you articulate the complete thought. (A sentence is a group of words that expresses a complete thought.)

It may feel like writing out your thoughts in full sentences is slowing you down, but in fact it's speeding you up. That's because when you write out a thought, you have a chance to consider it for a few seconds. You will automatically check, is it true? Or not? Often when I'm "thinking on paper," I'll notice a mistake and write, "no, that's not true," and then go on to sort out the issue. When you're confused or in conflict, you'd be surprised at how often there are falsehoods flitting through your head. "Thinking on paper" makes it easy to challenge them. And it's done naturally as you're transcribing your thinking in full sentences.

"Thinking on Paper" is particularly helpful when you're overloaded and going in circles.

1) You instantly become clearer on the separate issues, because you stop interrupting one thought with another. You have time to grasp the first problem before being bombarded with the second.

2) You stop going in circles, hearing the same six thoughts in rotation. After writing down those six, you have mental room to hear thoughts seven, eight, and nine. Those are the ones that will help you break out of the impasse.

3) You get clearer on what's important. As you write out a thought in a full sentence, you put it in the spotlight. Is it really true? How important is it right

now? Some of the issues on your mind are critical, some are irrelevant or mistaken. When you spell out each thought, you can better tell which is which.

We often look back and say, "I should have known that. Why didn't I think of that?" That's easy—it was out of mind. It takes a few seconds to trigger out-of-mind information from your databanks. But when you "think on paper," you give yourself the extra second or two to trigger crucial knowledge from your own memory banks. That information will guide you to a better decision.

FOUR GUIDELINES FOR THINKING ON PAPER

"Thinking on paper" means writing out your thoughts, in full sentences, as you think. Do it to help you do your best thinking and record your train of thought.

1. Start by writing down your **thinking goal**. Your objective is to figure out_____?

2. Record your thoughts **in full sentences**, following the main line of thinking. Slow down the thinking to match the pace of the writing.

3. Whenever you hesitate, write down a **helpful question** to get your thoughts moving on a path toward the goal. Then answer the question.

4. **Monitor** your progress and priorities and **redirect** as needed.

If you have a problem, stop to identify the exact problem. Then switch to thinking about a solution that would redirect you to a path toward the main goal.

TIPS:
- "Freewriting" is permitted. If you feel stuck, write

> down the words in your head, whatever they are, even if they seem off topic or not useful. This will help you clear out those ideas so you can eventually focus on the real issue.
> - Do not edit your thinking on paper or censor your thoughts. (This is particularly important if you are doing "thinking on paper" on a computer.)
> - Keep your "thinking on paper" private. Usually your thought process will not be clear to others. If you want to communicate the ideas to someone else, write up a summary of your conclusions.
> - If you get interrupted, finish your sentence. If possible, write two more sentences to yourself about how to pick up when you come back.

How long should you "think on paper"? Three minutes is usually enough time to raise any obvious issues, and solve 80% of the problems. If the problem is too large to solve in three minutes, then three minutes is enough time to figure that out—and decide what your next step should be.

If you've already wasted one minute in any kind of quandary or confusion, that three minutes of effort is definitely worth it. Your time savings can be huge. You immediately stop wasting time, and start thinking productively. Plus, you avoid that terrible ambivalent state in which work is going poorly, and you are easily tempted to procrastinate or chase after a distraction. Do this regularly, and you will find a lot more productive work fits into the day, without a lot more effort.

That's why I recommend the "3-minute rule" for "thinking on paper." At the first sign of trouble, on any task, big or small, pull out a piece of paper and do three minutes of "thinking on paper" to get yourself back on track. You'll be surprised at how quickly you can take stock of the situation and propel yourself into productive action.

Jean Moroney, President of Thinking Directions, believes that "smarter" is a learnable skill, and effort is a terrible thing to waste. She teaches managers, engineers, and other creatives how to solve problems faster, make better decisions, and find effective paths to their goals. Her practical approach draws on her background in Electrical Engineering (MIT BS '85, MS '86), augmented by Psychology (Carnegie-Mellon MS '92) and Philosophy (Ayn Rand Institute '96). Find out about her workshops, coaching programs, products and more at
www.thinkingdirections.com.
Contact her at jm@thinkingdirections.com.

BOOK FIVE:
YOUR POWER TO TAKE MORE TIME OFF

Power Time Management helps you have more time away from work to devote to vacations, family, friends and personal projects. You can do this by doubling productivity and streamlining your work efforts. In this section we'll cover these topics:

- Get More Time Off
- *Power Time Management* Based on Leverage
- Get More Done Through Momentum
- Power of the Crucial Action

GET MORE TIME OFF
(#1 of Take More Time Off)

Want more time away from work? We'll use the D.O.E.S. process (as in someone who *does* have more time off):

D - delegate
O – organize a speed up
E – encourage the "Activity-Recovery Pattern"
S – set a priority for rest

1. Delegate

In order to have more time to yourself, it helps to become an expert at delegating.

I'll share delegating methods in the form for work, but it's also helpful to have family members share household work, too. (For example, you can have children help clear an area by having drawers near the floor so that they can fill them.)

Here's a useful process: "Completed Staff Work." Train people who report to you to follow this procedure:

1. See a problem.

2. Come up with 3 solutions.

3. Endorse one and then go to the supervisor and explain your reasoning for endorsing the solution that you're recommending.

It's said that Napoleon had his generals use this 3-step method and then Napoleon was not plagued by people bothering him with things they could solve themselves.

Another important thing is to have a discussion and write down the following details:

1. What success at this task looks like.

2. A schedule that takes into account realities that the team member is facing.

For example, my company has paid interns. When I delegate work, I write notes in an email for the intern— while having a discussion with the intern. The email includes actual details about what needs to be accomplished and the due date. I send the email and soon after, the intern reads the notes and replies with additional comments or simply "got it."

In this way, I ensure that both the intern and I know what exactly we agreed to.

However, because most of my interns are students, I adjust my delegations according to the semester schedule. I take into account that at midterm and at the closing of the semester these students may need to be away from their internship work.

2. Organize a speed up

To have more time off, get more done when you're truly at work.

Go a bit faster, but do not rush so much that you create needless errors.

Make everything as simple as possible, but not simpler.
– Albert Einstein

From this quote, I take a pattern: **simplify AND acknowledge reality.**

Here's an important reality to face. We all have limitations on our time, and it's often important to choose what is "good enough."

For example, to speed up my writing process to complete a book, I make a plan and *Set Criteria for Excellence.*

Here are some details that I use with writing a book and Setting Criteria for Excellence

1. target 202 pages for the book.
2. work with two editors

3. first explore about half of the material of the book by writing about the topics in my blog articles

4. gather about 8 articles from best-selling authors to include their insights

The above 4 criteria help me *speed up* the completion of each book. This proves useful since this book that you're reading is my 24th book.

Quality is assured with two editors and my developing material over time in my blog articles.

To speed up your productivity, devise your own personal system.

3. Encourage the "Activity-Recovery Pattern"

Did you know that in a three-hour tennis match the pro tennis player is active only 20 minutes? Many top tennis coaches guide their players to be strategic with how they rest between bursts of activity. This is referred to in research as an *activity-recovery pattern*. When you know that you're going to have an intense 4-day period at work, schedule in rest and recovery to follow.

The big problem is that many people achieve a goal and then fail to stop and relish the good feeling. They just nod their head and jump into the next activity. No wonder they feel as if they are on a never-ending treadmill.

On the other hand, you can schedule your Recovery Time. You'll find that when you return to work you'll get more done and the quality will improve, too.

4. Set a priority for rest

Some time ago, I heard myself say, "I work seven days a week." I felt a momentary good feeling of "Look how dedicated I am."

But there's a problem with proclaiming how hard we work. Maybe it makes us feel special, but what it actually makes us is TIRED. And tired people make mistakes and they lack the energy to nurture relationships. That creates needless problems and wasted time.

To operate on a higher and more successful level, we need to set rest and recovery as a PRIORITY.

A well-rested person can think more clearly and be open to intuitive insight. That's valuable!

I invite you to consider taking off the "martyr's badge." Some parents, for example, proclaim, "Look how much I sacrifice for you." That's part of what I mean by "martyr's badge." It's as if "sacrifice for you" is some sort of equivalent for receiving a medal of honor.

Two things are going on here. Yes, there is value in being a dedicated parent. AND, it's great when parents do what is necessary to restore their own personal energy.

It begins with setting limits. For example, today I set a limit on how much writing time I was going to put in. I also have changed my own way of talking to myself about my schedule. Instead of proclaiming: "I work 7 days a week," I repeat this phrase to myself, "I work smart and enjoy fun and recovery. I'm well-rested and strong."

Now, I invite you to reflect on how you describe your own efforts and work habits. Consider doing what's necessary so that you're well-rested and strong.

Principle
Learn how to delegate and set up a personal Activity-Recovery Pattern.

Power Questions
Where can you put in breaks so that you can recover and

rest up? How might you delegate some work and relieve yourself of some stress?

* * *

To get more time off, you need to up the level of excellence in your habits. Better habits mean more productivity which can led to higher income and more time off. Now, we'll explore Patricia Fripp's insights about habits.

Do Your Habits Hurt or Help You?
by Patricia Fripp, CSP, CPAE

Good habits can determine our success in our public speaking, business communications, and even our careers. Our habits are part of us, built up like the layers of a pearl from our own juices. They can either provide a lustrous shield against adversity—or an imprisoning shell of our own making. **Just a few habits can make a big difference in both how we handle and how we project ourselves.** What new habits do you want to acquire? What old habits do you want to change? My brother, legendary guitarist Robert Fripp says, "Small additional increments are transformational."

Frippercize: Choose your habits…

Ask yourself:

- Which of my current habits help me?
- Which habits don't help me?
- What new habits do I want to acquire?
- Which habits will I get rid of?

You can continue doing comfortable things that don't work, or you can improve by learning and developing better habits. One of my co-presenters at The Lady & The Champs Speakers' Conferences, Craig Valentine says, "Without new tools and techniques you are just getting better at getting worse quicker."

Frippicism: "Tell me what you say you want; show me one week of your life and I will tell you if you will get it."

Portions of this article originally appeared in Patricia Fripp's book, *Get What You Want!*

Patricia Fripp, CSP, CPAE works with organizations and individuals who want to put their best foot forward by gaining powerful, persuasive, presentation skills. She is a Hall of Fame Keynote Speaker, Executive Speech Coach, and Sales Presentation Skills Expert.
 (415)753-6556, Fax (415)753-0914
 PFripp@ix.netcom.com, www.fripp.com
 www.fripp.com/blog/ twitter@Pfripp

* * * * * *

POWER TIME MANAGEMENT BASED ON LEVERAGE
(#2 of Take More Time Off)

Several years ago, I sent a book proposal to an agent who called me in less than one hour. I thought that I had hit a home run! Imagine my disappointment when he soon said we did not have a match. He talked about how my book project was too similar to others, but my intuition rang loud and clear: I did *not* have leverage. That was years before I was connected to thousands of people through LinkedIn, Facebook, Google+, Pinterest, Twitter and more. I had not written 24 books either.

Leverage in the publishing industry is about an author being able to sell her book and promote to thousands of contacts that she has *already* made. It's called "having a platform." It's also called having leverage.

Power Time Management is a way to streamline your journey to higher levels of success. A major element of such streamlining is to develop your personal leverage. We'll use the L.E.V.E.R. process:

L – learn "what's most important"
E – engage social media
V – verify the truth
E – entertain
R – respond quickly

1. Learn "what's most important"

Several years ago, Valentine's Day scared me. Why? I was deeply concerned about not getting the right gift.

Then I learned about two important questions:
- "What's most important to you about . . . ?"
- "What would make _____ a good experience for you?"

And then I took a crucial action. I asked my sweetheart, "What would make Valentine's Day a good experience for you?"

That's when I learned about the Fabulous Five (my term).

My sweetheart wants on Valentine's Day:

1. chocolate (a big surprise)
2. flowers
3. a greeting card
4. dinner
5. a balloon

So if I provide the Fabulous Five, I'm doing Valentine's Day right!

Here's how you develop a form of leverage based on having vital knowledge: Ask people the two powerful questions:

- "What's most important to you about . . .?"
- "What would make _____ a good experience for you?"

Then, when you can, take notes.

It's been reported that Bill Clinton successfully made his bid for becoming the U.S. President because he would study cards with personal information about people before he met with them again. Bill Clinton knew about people's children, their businesses, and other things that were most important to them.

How will you make sure that you ask questions and retain the information about what is most important to key people in your life?

By the way, here's another vital question to ask: "Who is your ideal client?" When you listen carefully to answers to this question, you can act like a *hub of influence*. Connect people. They'll remember you, and many will support you in return.

2. Engage social media

An individual artist needs only a thousand true fans in her tribe. It's enough. – Seth Godin, blogger (Time Magazine called

Seth's blog "one of the Top 25 blogs.")

Yes—one thousand true fans can do a lot! For example, the true fans of Joss Whedon and his one season show *Firefly* wielded such influence that TV/Film history was made. The failed *Firefly* TV show lived again as a major feature film *Serenity!*

Here's another example: One fan of Dr. Wayne Dyer helped him secure TV show interviews all over the United States at the beginning of Wayne's book writing career.

How do you get fans? You get busy on LinkedIn, Facebook, Google+, Twitter, Pinterest and other media platforms. Pinterest is powerful for attracting the attention of young women. For example, I worked with a new author who went from zero to having people from over 119 countries reading her blog. She looked at her statistics and saw that a large number of people were discovering her blog via Pinterest.

The secret of leadership is simple: Do what you believe in. Paint a picture of the future. Go there. People will follow. – Seth Godin

Currently, I am working with team members as I find ways to describe the innovation of my coaching efforts with clients. I realized that I am the only coach to combine these two things: *Your Secret Charisma* and *Power Time Management.*

I then started to mention that I provide: *The Charisma Advantage that Saves Time.*

Some of my advisors said, "I don't understand that. Charisma and time management don't go together."

I was undaunted. I replied, "Okay. I may need to find other words. But for something to be new, it will be unusual."

I went on to describe my process with a client:

"When I help you enhance your charisma, people trust you. And that saves time."

I shared my above personal example to show that it takes time, effort, and courage to find your own "voice."

When you engage social media, find a way to effectively *stand out* from the noise.

3. Verify the truth

To have real personal leverage, you need to find out the truth to what is going on behind the scenes.

When I started out in business, I spent a great deal of time researching every detail that might be pertinent to the deal I was interested in making. I still do the same today. People often comment on how quickly I operate, but the reason I can move quickly is that I've done the background work first, which no one usually sees. I prepare myself thoroughly, and then when it is time to move ahead, I am ready to sprint. – Donald Trump

Spectacular achievement is always preceded by unspectacular preparation. – Robert H. Schuller

Be sure to interview people who have already worked with someone you're contemplating aligning your future with. Do NOT fall for someone's sweet talk.

This is so important to me that I wrote two books about protecting yourself: *Darkest Secrets of Persuasion and Seduction Masters* and *Darkest Secrets of Negotiation Masters*.

Frankly, I was angry about the underhanded tricks some despicable people use. And I wanted to protect readers and help them get stronger.

I even wrote a book that pointed out how we must find out the truth for ourselves.

In my book, *Truth No One Will Tell You*, I wrote:

"There are the four reasons people fail to express the truth. These include:

1. They don't know the truth.
2. They don't want you to know the truth so they can exploit your weakness.
3. They care about you and want you to avoid getting hurt.
4. They can only guess about what is best for you because your inner truth is only revealed by your answers to effective questions.

An interviewer asked: "Which people are not telling the truth?" Many of us discover that, intentionally or not, the people who do not tell us the truth that could empower us include co-workers, family members, friends and politicians. Your life is truly in your hands."

When you do not know the truth and you make a decision, you get the opposite of positive leverage: you get slammed down.

So cultivate good relationships and good sources of information.

And practice listening to your intuition.

Sometimes, I share with my clients: "If you feel that you shouldn't get on an elevator with someone, then listen to your intuition! Some women think, 'Oh, I'm being silly.' We call these people—dead! Listen to your intuition."

Before you take a leap, verify the truth. At least, type in the name of a new company (for example) and check Google to see if "scam" or "problem" is associated with the company.

I once considered getting a new, adjustable bed. I read the reviews on Amazon.com and discovered to my shock that there was an uncomfortable wooden frame between the two people sleeping. Stop! If either person went across the center of the bed, they would feel the *thud* of hitting a rigid wooden frame.

I saved so much time and trouble by not getting that bed!

So read reviews and interview people. Get the information. Get the truth.

4. Entertain

People will pay more to be entertained than to be educated.
– Johnny Carson

Life is tough. As the old saying goes: "If anyone says life is not tough—they're either selling something or delusional."

So what do we, under so much stress, want? Some comfort. A respite. Some fun.

I still remember the song "Girls Just Wanna Have Fun."

See if you can help people feel good in your presence. How? Entertain them with a good story.

I'm not suggesting that you become a standup comedian. But it does help to practice your positive and interesting stories.

Avoid "poor me" stories and complaining.

I frequently use the phrase: "The good news is..." No matter how I may be feeling, I always have something positive to talk about.

Another way I entertain a person is to get them talking about something they feel good about.

Somewhere in the conversation I ask questions like:

- "So what are you looking forward to?"
- "Is there something going on that you like?"

When I get the other person to talk about something that is positive in their life, they enjoy themselves. In essence, they're entertaining themselves. And they appreciate that I'm a good audience for them.

When people feel good in your presence, you're developing good relationships. And good relationships are a source of excellent personal leverage.

For example, years ago, I wanted the URL Timepulse.com, but it was taken. My funds were dedicated elsewhere so I was not going to make a bid for that URL. Two years later, a friend noticed that Timepulse.com had been abandoned and contacted me. I said, "Thank you. And I'll call you back in about 10 minutes." I quickly registered TimePulse.com for my own company, and I have it to this day.

That's the power of developing good friendships.

5. Respond quickly

Several years ago, Al Gilbert, a man who closes $8 million dollar deals told me, "When someone leaves a voicemail, it's like a plea left in the wilderness."

The important thing is to reply to a voicemail quickly. Al would be on a plane, and he would make a phone call and say, "I'm on a plane into Chicago. When I get to the office, I'll look into that for you."

I've seen a number people fall into a bad habit. They, in essence, ignore an email or voicemail until they have a perfect answer. What they do not realize is that a potential customer has likely left a voicemail for three potential vendors. She is just waiting to see who gets back to her first.

You can reply quickly and say, "I got your voicemail. I'm

looking into those details. I'll likely have some information for you tomorrow afternoon."

At any given time, I'm in the middle of 19 email conversations. So I've developed a system for my contractors and interns. I have them reply to me with "got it" so that I know that they have the most recent, pertinent information.

When you want real personal leverage, respond quickly. For one thing, **people trust you** if they can count on you to respond quickly. It saddens me to see how a significant number of people are slow to respond to a voicemail or email. What they do not realize is that they're losing hundreds of leads for jobs and sales because they can't be trusted to respond quickly.

Think of it. Do you think Donald Trump hires contractors who are slow to respond? No way.

Be unusual. Be extremely trustworthy. How? Respond quickly.

* * *

Using the L.E.V.E.R. process, we streamline our journey to higher levels of success as we're perceived as both trustworthy and responsive. That's real Power Time Management.

Principle
Be sure to get the truth to make good decisions and to respond quickly to build vital relationships.

Power Question
How can you improve the way you communicate and respond quickly so that people can find you to be extremely trustworthy?

* * *

Since we talked about leverage, I'll share Jeanna Gabellini's insights about focusing on details that leverage your process to create new profits.

How To Jump Into a New Profit Bracket
by Jeanna Gabellini

I don't know about you, but I struggled mightily trying to figure out how to make a quantum leap. Funny thing is that anytime my profits jumped up in a significant way, it was never the way I had intended.

Does that mean that you can't plan for a big profit increase?

You can absolutely envision, plan and implement to see the exact results you desire, but there are some critical mindset strategies that must be included.

- **Don't make a big to-do about your current state of finances.** It is what it is. If your business has stayed in the same profit zone for twenty years, then make peace with it. Your resistance to "what is" keeps it your reality.
- **Look for the passionate idea first, profitability second.** Whenever you get attached to an idea because you think it is the only way to get out of your income rut, you can count on it not living up to your expectations. There is a level of emotional attachment to the idea, therefore aggravating your belief about scarcity. Desperation equals little movement up the wealth scale.
- **Play to win.** Go first class in your business

operations, delivery of your product and service and any marketing. I'm not talking about blowing your budget but you can't build something bigger without the infrastructure to support it. Hire the right people to do the right job. Put systems in place to make sure you pull off your plans effortlessly and leave plenty of time to do things in excellence. Skimping is cheap. Cheap means you're not ready to receive abundance.

- **Plan for profits.** Eliminate the words try, hope, if and maybe from your business conversations. You make a decision that this is the time, year, strategy, and launch that will deliver the results and don't hesitate as you move forward. You invest your passion and energy into your business knowing the pay off is 100% worth it.
- **Be.** Yep, just be. You don't move into a bigger income bracket from getting stuff done. When you slow down to ask the right questions, listen to your Inner Business Expert and do things intentionally, you'll do what you do with more impact. **BE**ing who you are, while you're doing stuff, will attract more profits.
- **Take action from your Guidance.** When the idea pops in your head, go for it. When a person, product, service, system or strategy feels like a HELL YES as soon as you think it, it IS the right move. Each step you take toward it will bring more clarity. You may later drop the idea because a better one pops in, but action creates the momentum you need to get to the next step.
- **Do not under estimate what you can create.** Anybody can make a business thrive once they've

committed to not staying where they are in the process. Commitment moves mountains. I've seen people double their clients with one idea. The idea wasn't what got them there. It was the mindset they were in before the idea.

Is this your year to move up the profit ladder? It is if you say it is. Put on your big girl/boy boots and kick some butt in the mindset department. The ideal strategies, mentors, resources and ideas will literally land in your lap. Your job is to say YES.

Jeanna Gabellini is a Master Business Coach who supports conscious entrepreneurs to double (and even triple) their profits by leveraging attraction principles, proven strategies and fun. She is also the co-author of *Life Lessons for Mastering the Law of Attraction*, with Eva Gregory, Mark Victor Hansen & Jack Canfield. And her newest book: *10 Minute Money Makers: How to Easily Double Your Profits in Just 10 Minutes a Day!*

Combining vision, divine guidance and easy to implement actions, Jeanna delivers top-tier private coaching & sold-out seminars that have allowed committed entrepreneurs to blow past their self-imposed limits, ditch the drama of overwhelm and move into radical joy, inner peace and ever-increasing profits.

www.MasterPEACEcoaching.com

* * * * * *

GET MORE DONE THROUGH MOMENTUM
(#3 of Take More Time Off)

Would you like to get more done and feel better doing it? Working with clients, I emphasize: "Momentum Makes Miracles." We'll use the C.A.N. process:

C – clear distractions
A – arrange "the start"
N – nurture great timing

1. Clear distractions
Cheryl feels squeezed by responsibilities both at work and with family. She gets into the habit of doing two things at once. She'll talk on the phone while sitting with her son and playing a game of checkers. She'll write an email while responding to a phone call at work.

Recent research has demonstrated that multi-tasking is NOT doing two things at once. It is really "rapid starts and stops." That is, if one is typing an email and talking on the phone at the same time, one's brain is starting to type the email and quickly stopping one's attention to the phone call. And then one is quickly taking attention off the email and putting it back to the phone conversation. Several researchers conclude that it is NOT more efficient to do two things at once. The person is actually using up more brain energy than necessary. Actual lab results show that the person who "multi-tasks" actually does the two things with less precision and less effectiveness. Not good.

"Clearing distractions" can be as simple as turning off a chime that rings each time email arrives in your inbox. For many people, that chime interrupts their train of thought. Then they may lose their momentum. Worse: they have to gear up (and lose time doing it) to get back to where they were in the project.

Another example: Much of my work is creative so I have times in the day in which I turn off the ringer on my cell phone. I do NOT want to have my creativity and my momentum on a project to be interrupted.

2. Arrange "the start"
Inspiration usually comes during work rather than before it.
– Madeleine L'Engle

As a professional writer, I frequently press on and start working on a writing project no matter how I feel. Several times a month, I start writing and I immediately do not like the first few paragraphs. I think, "This is not good enough." But I press on anyway. Often, five minutes into continuing my writing, I finally start to see material that I actually like. As top author Madeleine L'Engle advises: Inspiration usually comes during work rather than before it.

So my point is: Simply start. Do NOT wait for inspiration. Do NOT wait to "feel like doing" the task.

Do you need to make headway on your taxes paperwork? Simply start by laying the folders out on your desk. Just concentrate on that small step to just start. Consider using the words "Just Start" as a form of mantra to get you going.

I keep a log of the writing I complete during the day. I focus on my phrase: *Keep Score and Achieve More*. I just start by looking at the log and seeing yesterday's progress.

3. Nurture great timing
Find your "Best Moments" during the day. For me, the first moments after awakening are "prime time." I avoid answering email at this time. I avoid calling a friend. I simply sit down and start writing. Often as I'm waking up,

my subconscious mind is serving up new ideas and good ideas that I want to immediately type into my current writing project (like this book). My family knows that I will not come down and eat first when I wake up in the morning. I often start writing and after completing some work—then I'll take a break and have breakfast.

That's my process. Find your own Best Moments.

Secondly, for your great timing, effectively incorporate breaks in your schedule. With an appropriate break, you'll be surprised how refreshed you feel and how much momentum you'll have on a project upon your return.

For example, one of my friends has been away from creative work for a number of months. Then she rearranged her schedule and cleared some time. Suddenly, she's now writing a book, writing songs and drawing illustrations for two children's books. She calls it "a miracle." Truly her time away from creativity was, for her, a revving up time. At this point, it's time for her to nurture her momentum. Perhaps, she'll limit some of her social activities so that she can take advantage of her momentum and churn out a lot of creative work.

Remember: **Momentum Makes Miracles.**

Principle
Momentum makes miracles.

Power Question
How can you support your own momentum?

* * *

Getting started generates momentum. As Jeanna Gabellini shares in the next article, get started and you do not need money to achieve many great outcomes.

Don't Wait for the Money
by Jeanna Gabellini

It's normal to put off things in life until you have the money to do them. But does it have to be that way?

Absolutely not!

Never wait until the money shows up or you'll spend most of your time waiting. And while you wait, you'll be thinking about the many things for which you are waiting. You'll be filled with a feeling of longing. It's not empowering.

You've got to make a decision to have what you want now. Then, the money will show up or you'll be able to enjoy what you wanted in a way you hadn't expected.

And you can enjoy what you have now, and be in eager anticipation for what is coming down the pipe.

There have been many times in my life when the money to travel was not present. Yet, my desire to travel was always burning. Once I learned that the Universe responds to my decisions, I made the decision to always find a way to travel. And I have.

Here are some of the ways I was supported in traveling without creating financial debt to do it:
- Friends and family invited me to stay at their vacation homes.
- When I made airplane reservations, I got unexpected deals.
- I was upgraded in hotels and airline seats without even requesting it.
- My mom shared her timeshare with me.

- I created ideal trips to places where I had friends with whom I could stay.
- I got new clients within a week of deciding to take a trip.
- I found ways to experience my desire for adventure locally.

Once you make a decision to have whatever it is you want, the way to have it reveals itself quickly. Making a decision may seem a bit crazy when the money isn't there, but it is exactly this process that brings the prosperity to you.

Yes, it takes faith that you will find a way to have what you want. **The cool part is that you don't always need to figure out how you'll do it before you make the decision.**

I remember deciding to buy my BMW M3. I didn't have a clue how to come up with the down payment for the car, but I felt that the car was already mine when I left the dealership to think about a way to create the money. Within 24 hours I knew how to get the car and within a month I created the down payment from "nowhere."

Up to that point in my life, I'd never created that much money in such a short time and so spontaneously. The decision to buy the car drew the money to me like bees to honey. It was easy. I wasn't scared about finding a way to buy the car. I was simply excited to have the car.

Decisions are solid, unlike a wish. What do you need to make a decision about? Are you on the fence about an investment for your business? Waiting to buy a home? Need help with your website?

Make a move. What's one small step you can take to say YES to the thing you've been waiting for?

Jeanna Gabellini is a Master Business Coach who supports conscious entrepreneurs to double (and even triple) their profits by leveraging attraction principles, proven strategies and fun. She is also the co-author of *Life Lessons for Mastering the Law of Attraction*, with Eva Gregory, Mark Victor Hansen & Jack Canfield. And her newest book: *10 Minute Money Makers: How to Easily Double Your Profits in Just 10 Minutes a Day!*

Combining vision, divine guidance and easy to implement actions, Jeanna delivers top-tier private coaching & sold-out seminars that have allowed committed entrepreneurs to blow past their self-imposed limits, ditch the drama of overwhelm and move into radical joy, inner peace and ever-increasing profits.

www.MasterPEACEcoaching.com

* * * * * *

POWER OF THE CRUCIAL ACTION
(#4 of Take More Time Off)

Imagine that you could identify what would most benefit your career. It's probably the task you're most dreading. And there's another thing: this task would likely catapult your success and ultimately give you more opportunities to take time off.

Then, why do we procrastinate? And worse yet, some of us never do this crucial task that could transform our careers.

With my clients and college students, I emphasize:

Often the thing we dread the most is the best for our career.

My clients name that "thing I dread most":
- making marketing calls
- calling people to get them to pay my bill
- updating my resume
- attending networking events
- negotiating so that I have excellent compensation for the work I do for the client
- rehearsing so that I can close the sale during my next sales meeting

How can we get ourselves to do the dreaded task? The answer is to do the task when you have the most willpower and energy. That's earlier in the day. The shortcut to this idea is: **Worst First.**

Do what you dread near the beginning of the day and you take advantage of your strongest willpower. Willpower has been compared to a muscle. By the end of the day, the "willpower muscle" is fatigued. (Ever eat perfectly at breakfast time but have three doughnuts at 11 pm?) This observation is supported by research conducted at Stanford University and elsewhere.

I use this knowledge of *Worst First* in two ways.

I start my day by writing no matter how I'm feeling. I do not wait for inspiration. As a professional writer, I put my rear in the chair and start writing. Many times it's painful because I can see that I'm not writing well. But around five minutes into the process, I start writing better and better.

The second way I use Worst First is: *I eat salad for breakfast.*

Now, I have some questions for you:

Do you need to update your resume? Pull out a sheet of paper or open a file now. Now? Yes, get started.

Do NOT wait to get inspired.

Do you need to do some money-related paperwork? Start

now.

Some salespeople make their first marketing phone call in the morning and then have a bite to eat or a drink of coffee.

Here's another application of **Worst First.** If you have a presentation to do at the end of the week, rehearse for 9 minutes every morning. This *9-Minute Rehearsal* done each day for 4 days will do more for you than cramming for 3 hours on one day. Why? Your subconscious mind will work on your presentation during the rest of the day after you've accomplished your morning 9-Minute Rehearsal.

* * *

Worst First is one of the most useful methods that I've employed to help me write 24 books.

I invite you to take this method "for a test drive." You'll see your productivity rise.

Principle

Identify some important task that you're dreading and then practice *Worst First*—take action on it early in the day.

Power Questions

What are three tasks that you dread a great deal? How can you take some action—even for just 10 minutes—early in the day?

* * *

For many of us, there is a crucial action that may be ignoring. Now, Rebecca Morgan reveals that particular action.

Are You Joyful at Work?

by Rebecca Morgan, CSP, CMC

What do dancers at a Sikh celebration in Kuala Lumpur, Malaysia and happy employees have in common?

They show their happiness.

Granted, not all employees are as exuberant as these dancers, whose sincere grin decorated their faces throughout their performance. Some people are happy but don't let their face know.

However, the glee of the men performing at the celebration I attended was infectious. I marveled at how truly delighted they seemed to be at showing us their moves. Unlike a previous dance group at the same event, whose smiles seemed to painted on, these men's faces matched their enthusiastic steps.

Are you gleeful at work? Some might think it's inappropriate to show anything but a somber business-like face. But if you exude your pleasure of the work you're doing and the people you're with, it's bound to spread.

Yes, there will be the naysayers, those who are unhappy in their own lives, and will look askance at any display of cheerful enthusiasm, labeling their chipper coworkers as brown nosers, cheerleaders, or Polyannas. If you are the subject of such backlash know that you've elicited jealousy from those who aren't as free with their positiveness.

Watching the dancers ebullient dancing made me smile broadly. It was a delight to watch people who were sincerely enjoying what they do. It reminded me to show more joyousness in my work.

Rebecca L. Morgan, CSP, CMC, specializes in creating innovative solutions for customer service challenges. She's appeared on 60 Minutes, Oprah, the *Wall Street Journal*,

National Public Radio and *USA Today*. Rebecca is the bestselling author of 25 books, including *Calming Upset Customers* and *Professional Selling*. She is an exemplary resource who partners with you to accomplish high ROI on your strategic customer service projects. For information on her services, books, and resources, or for permission to repost or reprint this article, contact her at 408/998-7977, Rebecca@RebeccaMorgan.com, http://www.RebeccaMorgan.com/

* * *

The crucial action, that Rebecca implies, is that **we actively look for ways to enjoy ourselves at work.** Just for moments here and there. I know that when I coach a client, I fill up with joy that I'm supporting the person to increase their feelings of joy and fulfillment. And, I let the person hear my joy in my voice (on the phone) and in my voice and face when in person. Enthusiasm is contagious.

BOOK SIX:
YOUR POWER TO INCREASE HAPPINESS AND LOVING RELATIONSHIPS

Power Time Management helps you focus on those things that increase happiness. Research data suggests that numerous people find that 80% of their happiness arises from relationships so it helps to improve skills in relationship-building. In this section we'll cover these topics:

- *Power Time Management* to Increase Happiness
- Save Time and Save Yourself from Heartache
- Reduce Stress and Save Time
- Soulful Time Management
- Discover Hidden Secrets of Your Relationships and Create Closeness

POWER TIME MANAGEMENT TO INCREASE HAPPINESS
(#1 of Increase Happiness and Enhance Relationships)

Would you like to increase the times when you feel happy? I learned much about happiness by observing "Gertrude," one of the most miserable people I've met. Gertrude's life is marked by frustration and emptiness. She would do well to focus on this quote:

"Rules for Happiness: Something to do, Someone to love, Something to hope for." – Immanuel Kant

When it comes to time management, check your schedule. Are you devoting time to all three elements—something to do, someone to love and something to hope for?

Now, we'll explore the H.A.P.P.Y. process:

H - help
A - allow
P – prepare to let go
P – participate in love
Y – yield to gratitude

1. Help

I don't know what your destiny will be, but one thing I know: the only ones among you who will be really happy are those who will have sought and found how to serve. – Albert Schweitzer

One day when reflecting, I realized one source of

Gertrude's unhappiness is that she does not have anyone to serve!

Many of us discover that we really enjoy life while being kind to others.

If you want other people to be happy, practice compassion.
If you want to be happy, practice compassion. – The Dalai Lama

Many people who gain a quick, large inflow of money discover that merely hopping from one pleasurable activity to another ultimately becomes tiresome. On the other hand, it's great to have someone to be kind to. This ties in with both something to do and someone to love.

2. Allow

When I speak of "allow," I'm talking about "Allow this moment to be as it is." Another way to say this is: **"It is what it is."**

If we are screaming against a typhoon, it does nothing for us and makes no difference to the typhoon.

However, we can look on the present moment as an orange. Squeeze the orange and get orange juice.

In a sense, *allow the orange to be an orange* and stop complaining that the orange is not a cranberry.

Here is another thing to allow: *Allow that you'll want to go for something more.*

One way to view this is: **Allow that you can enjoy this moment *and* still go for more.**

I'd rather say, *"Go for different."*

I read a case history in which a boy truly enjoyed playing with one blue toy car. His grandmother saw the boy's delight, so she bought him 10 more cars. Soon the boy tired of playing with ANY toy cars. What happened here? With one blue car, the toy was precious. With many more cars, the preciousness was squeezed out of the situation.

The above case history inspires me to continue with my plan to "Go for different" instead of merely going for more.

3. Prepare to let go

Let go of preconceptions.

For example, before I completed my first feature film, I had a preconception of how I would feel on the day of completion. I thought I'd literally jump for joy and feel like I had just soared into the best chapter of my life!

What I learned is: *whatever your preconception, the end result or experience is going to be different.*

On the day of completing my first feature film, I smiled when I realized we were done. Then I just sat back, exhausted.

I did not feel the total elation that I expected to arrive upon hitting the big milestone.

Since that time, I've learned that my happiness is supported when I enjoy each moment as it flows along.

Holding onto big preconceptions and big expectations can lead to disappointment.

I've also learned to enjoy the process because accomplishments feel like brief resting moments. I do not live there.

I flow forward to what interests me.

You can act to change and control your life; and the procedure, the process is its own reward. – Amelia Earhart

Enjoy the process. Find an activity which you feel is intrinsically rewarding.

4. Participate in love

Your task is not to seek for love, but merely to seek and find all the barriers within yourself that you have built against it. – Rumi

I've discovered that I feel love the most when I participate in it *as I do something loving* for my loved one.

I've also learned to let go of strictly focusing on what someone can do for me.

Some of my happiest moments include wrapping a present for my sweetheart. It's the act of doing something for her that brightens my day.

It's been noted that marriage is a place *you go to give,* not just to get.

Remember the detail that happiness is "someone to love." And notice that it's NOT "happiness is just getting goodies from someone who loves you."

Participate in love.

5. Yield to gratitude

I use the word "yield" with care. In a sense, we need to "give in" to what is present here and now.

The current situation may not be ideal, but there is much to be grateful for.

I remember the day my mother suddenly took ill. I was in another part of the state of California. I travelled to the city where she resides with my father.

I took her hand when I arrived at her bedside.

Here's the unusual detail: to me, it was not a "bad day." It was a day that had some "bumpy moments." Sure, I felt worried. But I focused on being present with my mother in the moment.

I had much to be grateful for:

- My mother had access to excellent medical care.
- I had the means to travel to her side.
- My sweetheart was going with me, so I had her support.

I invite you to squeeze this present moment like an orange and get the juice. One way is to say to yourself, "I am grateful for. . ." and express 10 things you're grateful for in this present moment.

* * *

As we see from the H.A.P.P.Y. process, happiness is multi-faceted. And apparently, it includes letting go of preconceptions, expectations and feelings of "give stuff to me!"

Participate in the present moment. Remember: "Happiness is something to do, someone to love and something to hope for."

To really practice Power Time Management and to increase feelings of fulfillment, you need to take action and schedule activities that support all three: "something to do, someone to love and something to hope for."

Here is an item related to "something to hope for": schedule in tasks that "build something." Build a warm relationship. Build a second career. Build a friendship by helping another person rehearse for an important event.

Enjoy the moment, build for the future, live in the now.

Principle

Happiness is something to do, someone to love and something to hope for.

Power Question

How will you take specific actions to support "something to do, someone to love and something to hope for" today and every day?

* * * * * *

SAVE TIME AND SAVE YOURSELF FROM HEARTACHE
(#2 of Increase Happiness and Enhance Relationships)

Several years ago, my heart raced because I was holding a new girlfriend as we zoomed down the flume ride of Splash Mountain at Disneyland! A couple of months later, my heart was flattened as I composed a musical piece entitled: "Why Does Your Cat Get More Loving?"

The title of the song and my feelings that inspired it were clues to how upside down the situation was. You see, I could sense that something was wrong.

But the questions were: Would I look at the reality of my then-love relationship? Would I have the tough conversation with her?

Ultimately I learned the power of this question:

"What truth do you need to face?"

The title of this section is "Save Time and Save Yourself from Heartache." We might say, "Save yourself from extra and prolonged heartache." The truth was: the longer I persisted in avoiding the tough conversation, the longer I would feel this ache in my heart about a relationship that was not working.

Now, I invite you to pull out a sheet of paper or your

journal and write at the top of the page: *What truth do you need to face?*

Start writing. Do not censor your words. If you feel that you don't have anything to write, start with: "I don't have anything to write, but if I did I would talk about . . ."

It may seem strange, but merely acknowledging your in-the-moment experience and adding "but if I did . . ." can actually loosen up your thinking and allow you to see new facets or elements of your journey through life.

The question "What truth do you need to face?" relates to confronting the reality of one's current situation. Along this line . . .

Power Time Management includes:
- facing reality
- feeling what you need to feel
- grieving when necessary
- making a plan to do something that supports you in living as "your best self"
- taking action.

It really begins with an ultimately *empowering* question: "What truth do you need to face?"

Here's what happened with my then-girlfriend.

I told her how I felt that things were off and perhaps, this relationship was not working.

Her response surprised me. It included her comment, "I would have continued for another six months."

What?!

Another six months of living a lie?

Wow! Facing the reality of the relationship saved me six months!

Now that's Power Time Management!

Principle
Ask yourself "What truth do I need to face?"—and discover what needs to be improved upon.

Power Question
How will you make space to take a few moments to face reality by using the question "What truth do I need to face?"

* * * * * *

REDUCE STRESS AND SAVE TIME!
(#3 of Increase Happiness and Enhance Relationships)

Want less stress? Of course! Let's make a first distinction. There are things in our life that are simply tough to deal with. However, our thought patterns can either make our experience of stress better or worse. An old phrase is: "Pain is inevitable. Suffering is optional." This section is about reducing the suffering. We'll use the N.O.W. process:

N - nurture
O – open to Replacements for Time-Wasters
W – win in some way on a daily basis

1. Nurture
Where do you live moment to moment? This question may sound strange, but it's referring to the dominant focus of your thoughts. Are you stuck in worries about things that may happen? Then you're "living in the future."

Are you focused on regrets for things in your past? Then you're "living in your past."

The truth is: It's more stressful to live in either the future or the past.

The solution is to bring your attention to the present moment.

To do that you need to relieve some basic forms of pain.

Some people focus on H.A.L.T. (hungry, angry, lonely, tired) as a memory device to double-check their current state of being.

Simply put, take care of yourself—that is, nurture yourself—so that you're not stuck in one of these painful states: hungry, angry, lonely or tired.

Nurture yourself, and you think more clearly and have more resources.

When you have full access to your clear thinking, you can reduce your stress in this present moment.

2. Open to Replacements for "Time-Wasters"

A major source of reducing stress is to open your thoughts to new ideas. Also, open your awareness to Time-Wasters, which include people, things, or even your own personal habits that waste your time.

Here are examples and solutions:

a) Someone takes up time by gossiping at work.

Solution: Get up from your desk and meet the gossiper at your office door. Say, "Oh, I was just going to do something. Was there something real quick that you were going say?" After they respond, you give a brief reply and then walk out of your own door. You say, "Well, I've got to get back to work. See you." And you walk away.

b) Watching too much television, spending too much time on Facebook or with online gaming.

Solution: Set a timer. If you need support, call a friend and say, "I'm going to set a timer. I'll send you an email when I've successfully stopped watching TV or stepped away from my online game. You'll be like my coach, and my email to you will be my way of being 'accountable.' Thanks."

The pattern that works is for you to *set up Replacement Behaviors in place of Time-Wasters.*

3. Win in some way on a daily basis

How do many of us experience stress? By feeling frustration, anger and fear.

Where do such upset feelings come from? Loss. Either we're experiencing a real loss in the moment or we're remembering a previous loss. We might even focus on the fear of something happening in the future.

To reduce feelings of stress or upset, think of focusing your mind.

Nothing contributes so much to tranquilize the mind as a steady purpose—a point on which the soul may fix its intellectual eye. – Mary Wollstonecraft Shelley

How can you connect with that steady purpose? How can you tranquilize your mind?

Focus on having a Personal Victory each day. It works best if you have a Personal Victory in the morning. Then you start your day feeling good. Such good feelings empower you the rest of the day.

Some people feel good about using their treadmill for 10 minutes in the morning.

A writer might write for 20 minutes before getting into the shower.

I suggest you find something in your day so that you can "Make it a game you can win."

Here's an example. For this book, I planned on writing two separate sections "reduce stress" and "save time." But my editors noted that the book was getting too long to fit my readers' usual preferences.

I made a decision in line with "make it a game you can win." I decided to combine the sections into what you're now reading. In this way, I reduced stress and saved my time!

Now I invite you to do similar actions. Ask yourself: **"How can I make this a game I can win?"**

Principle
Find a way to have a Personal Victory on a daily basis.

Power Questions
How can you incorporate a Personal Victory into each day? Is there something you can modify so that you can "make it a game you can win"?

* * *

Having a Personal Victory each day will invigorate you with positive energy. In addition, we need to actively reduce our distress level. Dr. Elayne Savage now provides insights about these details.

Outraged, Then Enraged, Then Road Raged
By Elayne Savage, Ph.D.

A driver comes from out of nowhere, slows down to a crawl, cuts you off, tailgates, or flashes their lights.

It feels like an invasion of your personal space. Words or obscene gestures are exchanged; it starts getting out of hand. Before you know it you're becoming outraged, then enraged, then road raged.

Raging on the road is an overreaction to feeling wronged, slighted, or intruded on. Our personal space feels invaded. Before we know it, we're feeling "dissed." Next we are taking it personally and retaliating. One minute we feel like a victim. Then next, we become victimizer.

Feeling "dissed" pops up in a multitude of makes and models. Feeling "dissed" means feeling disrespected, of course. But do you know there are dozens of "words beginning with "dis" that describe feeling rejected in some way?

Being "dissed might mean feeling "disrespected," "dismissed," "displaced," "discredited," "disregarded," "discarded," "disposable," "dishonored," or "disenfranchised." When you consider the intense emotions evoked, no wonder anger rises to the surface so quickly. Before you know it, the rage builds up. Road rage has the same intensity as all other kinds of rages. AND it comes equipped with a built in weapon—your car.

My definition of rage is "anger with a history." Rage is an emotion far beyond anger. Anger relates to something happening in the present and reflects "now" feelings. By contrast, rage arises from overwhelming, often unbearable feelings from the past. It is attached to our childhood history or life experiences.

A distressing event in the present becomes unbearable when it reminds us of painful experiences from the past. Before we know it, an out-of-control reaction gets triggered. Old injustices stockpile into a repository of rage, just waiting to be disgorged. And once expelled, it contaminates our surroundings.

By considering rage in a larger context, we can gain some perspective. Then we don't have to feel so helpless in the face of our reaction.

Road Rage as Metaphor

Let's take a look at how road rage may reflect past injustices. Do you recall all those times you were hurt by others' insensitive behavior? The times you endured being "cut off," "squeezed out," "ignored," "kept waiting," "pushed around," "bumped" or "edged out." When a similar experience is recreated in the present, that old stockpile of hurts ignites. We overreact. It's easy to become enraged.

By recognizing the appearance of these metaphors we can better understand road rage. For example, how might you react when a driver suddenly drifts into your lane without a warning or signal? Does it feel like an invasion of your personal space? Does it offend your sensibilities? Do you fume? Do you want to retaliate?

"Don't Pick On Me!"

Often the incident triggers a not-so-pleasant childhood memory. Suddenly you find yourself back in grade school, remembering how the class bully used to taunt you, or push in front of you in the lunch line. You probably hated that feeling of helplessness. Maybe you yearned to defend your territory but didn't know how. Maybe you still cringe at the indignity of feeling victimized.

Now, on the road, that clueless person cuts in front of you and those old feelings get triggered. Revenge fantasies appear out of nowhere, "Boy, are they going to be sorry."

Are You Turning into the Bully You Detest?

It is amazing what the cloak of anonymity of the car can do. Before you know it you are turning into the bully you detest. But when you think about it, bullies are not really feeling very powerful. Under that aggressive exterior is usually a scared, hurting, ineffectual person.

When we feel vulnerable, we tend to protect ourselves by taking a tough stance. We engage in rageful or bullying behavior. We puff ourselves up. We act out our rage on the offending driver who doesn't understand that we are retaliating against all the bullies from our childhood. We may even seek out an unsuspecting person to bully back.

It happens so fast—something gets triggered and we lose control. We get confused and can't sort out or feelings. Before we know it, we're behaving badly. How can this be happening? We see ourselves as kind and considerate. How can we be behaving so outrageously on the road?

But, then again, our behavior may merely be a reflection of the outrageous times in which we live. We have to learn to live with it, but we also have to learn to control it.

You may find if you dwell on what happened on the road, it gets carried into your personal relationships and affects your concentration and productivity at work. Why take a chance on this negative energy ruining your day or week? Take back your power and reclaim your energy by using these tips:

Tips for Dealing with Road Rage

- If you are being raged at on the road, don't bite the bait, don't engage. A confrontation is only going to be a lose-lose situation for you. You might get hurt.
- The next time someone cuts you off, remind yourself there's a difference between an aggressive

driver and an inconsiderate or careless driver.

- Put the incident in perspective by remembering the metaphor theory. Ask yourself what old feelings this incident is re-creating for you.
- Take a breather. Ten slow breaths can work wonders to reduce stress.
- Most importantly, don't take it personally! Chances are the other driver's careless mistakes are not directed at you.

Elayne Savage, PhD, is a marriage and family therapist, communication and workplace coach and professional speaker in Berkeley, CA. She is the author of two books published in nine languages: *Don't Take It Personally! The Art of Dealing with Rejection* and *Breathing Room—Creating Space to Be a Couple* (New Harbinger Publications, iUniverse).
www.queenofrejection.com
For more communication tips:
Blog: 'Tips from The Queen of Rejection'®
Twitter@ElayneSavage
LinkedIn.com/in/elaynesavage

* * *

Dr. Elayne reminds us to use ten slow breaths to help us calm down. I'll add that it truly helps to nurture yourself daily. Be sure to take good care of yourself and beware of H.A.L.T. (hungry, angry, lonely, tired) and do something to take care of your needs. Stay strong. Stay refreshed.

* * * * * *

SOULFUL TIME MANAGEMENT
(#4 of Increase Happiness and Enhance Relationships)

Soulful Time Management includes developing your feelings of happiness and inner peace by connecting with your Divine Gifts. I first shared these gifts in my book *10 Seconds to Wealth*. We'll use what I call the D.I.V.I.N.E. process:

1. Decide (love)
2. Intuit (humility)
3. Voice (forgiveness)
4. Inspire (faith)
5. Nurture (grace)
6. Express (art)

As an introduction, consider the benefits and opportunities of these six Divine Gifts.

1. Love. You feel energized and on purpose while expressing love. While sharing love, you feel full of life and connected with people and Higher Power beyond yourself. Life has meaning. You don't need to have a romantic partner in that you can experience love by expressing kindness to people you interact with daily.

2. Humility. Listening to new ideas. Not just hearing, actually listening. Simply stated, learning from others, growing by being around them, gaining skills you might not have realized even existed! You value your intuition to guide you along your unique path.

3. Forgiveness. The burden lifts. When forgiving—not only others but yourself—the cycle of blame and punishment breaks down. You recover not simply strength and joy but also freedom.

4. Faith. You feel supported, no longer alone. You come to an understanding of suffering, and with that you feel a patience with which to face life's hardships.

5. Grace. You become open to receiving Divine help. You go beyond surviving to thriving. You notice that you're blessed on a daily basis. Just recall the times when you were in a situation in which a traffic accident almost happened, but somehow everything turned out well and you and all the nearby drivers were safe. That's a moment in which some of us feel touched by grace. Explore three facets of grace:

a) Grace is unmerited favor from Higher Power.
b) Grace is a grateful approach to every moment.
c) Grace is approaching each moment with elegance and refinement of movement or speech.

6. Art. Express yourself, finding joy in that expression. We create literally all the time. With every word, every movement, each thought you're creating the next moment's experience.

1. Decide (love)

To love is to be happy with. – Barry Neil Kaufman

Soulful Time Management is about staying in the moment and doing that which enriches and enlivens your

soul.

It's really about making good decisions. And it's also about saving time by avoiding falling down into a negative spiral of thoughts and feelings.

Two elements that help in making loving decisions: be supportive and humble.

For example, we may have a vivid idea of what we think is best for a loved one to do. However, we're *not* in their shoes. What we can do to be supportive is to be present as the loved one makes his or her decisions.

One colleague mentioned this years ago: "There's a difference between 'helping' and 'serving.' Some people think they're helping by pushing their ideas on someone. On the other hand, serving another is about asking: 'How can I be supportive to you? How would you prefer I support you?'"

A clear example relates to talking with a loved one.

Often, I ask: "Would you like me to just listen? Or would you like me to brainstorm ideas with you?" Several times, the person will say, "Just listen."

That's serving your loved one.

It can be a tough decision. Why? Because, for many of us, it's too painful to just watch as a loved one goes through struggles. But the truth is: people change or don't change on *their* schedule.

We seek to support, not push. Often, pushing just results in pushing the loved one away.

So we decide *for* love. We decide to be patient and to support in the way the other requests.

2. Intuit (humility)

Humility is not thinking less of yourself, it's thinking of yourself less. – C. S. Lewis

In a number of books, I've written about my term *Healthy Humility*. The term is about *not* thinking of yourself as better than others, nor as less than others. Healthy Humility is about taking your place with your fellow humans and participating in service, kindness and compassion.

For example, I'll think about my writing a book as "this is God's book, I'm participating." I'm writing the book, and I have editors and graphic designers on my team. We do this project together.

Here's another important part of humility: the ability to admit a mistake. Can you trust someone who never admits to making a mistake? No. Why? If someone cannot admit any errors, he or she cannot learn and cannot be coached to do better. **Being coachable, having that form of humility, is essential to being trustworthy.**

Another aspect of Healthy Humility is about welcoming intuitive thoughts. Some of us believe that we're gifted with intuitive thoughts and guidance from Higher Power. If that is so, we'll do better if we *listen*.

I always remember this quote:

We must be willing to relinquish the life we've planned in favor of the life that is waiting for us. – Joseph Campbell

I've had moments of humility when I was so grateful that my first thought was incorrect and that life turned out better than my first preference. For example, I remember feeling devastated and heartbroken at the end of my first romantic relationship. My dream was dashed. But one year later, I learned more about that former lover, and I realized: "God, you saved me from that one! Thank you!"

So humility can support us in feeling grateful *and* happy.

3. Voice (forgiveness)

Forgiveness is ending the cycle of blame and suffering.
– Dr. Fred Luskin

The above quote from Dr. Fred is one that he shared on a television show for which we both served as guest experts. I've always remembered Dr. Fred's comment.

Don't carry a grudge; while you're carrying a grudge, the other guy's out dancing. – Buddy Hackett

So don't carry a grudge.
Do create a plan.

Having a plan is valuable in the situation when you'd like forgiveness from another person.

Such a plan would include some elements I shared in my book *Your Secret Charisma: How to Repair Business and Personal Relationships—and Gain Trust and Forgiveness for Success, Happiness and Fulfillment.*

In that book, I shared the F.A.R. process:

"To make it easy to remember, I refer to the F.A.R. process:

- Forgiveness—ask for **forgiveness.**
- Amends—seek to make **amends.**
- Regret—express your **regret.**"

To encourage a loved one to grant forgiveness, one can use a plan like this:

- Once a week, ask for forgiveness.
- Three times a week, express your regret.
- Four times a week, take action to make amends.

Forgiveness involves voicing our concern and our resolve to do better.

4. Inspire (faith)

Change the way you look at things and the things you look at change. – Dr. Wayne Dyer

Recently, I learned that we can inspire ourselves. How? During a recent conversation, I witnessed that two friends had different views of the idea of karma, which includes the thoughts of cause and effect. A number of people say, "Karma means that if I do good, good things happen to me."

One of my friends used a metaphor. She said, "When I do something good, it's like dropping a rock in a cement pond. Ripples extend out from the splashing rock and bounce off the edge of the cement pond. The ripples of goodness return to me multiplied."

My other friend, "George," said, "I do something good, and it just goes out into the lake and just dissipates."

This is where faith comes in. My first friend has faith that the universe is ultimately benevolent with blessings multiplied.

My other friend, George, holds no such faith.

Faith is taking the first step even when you don't see the whole staircase. – Martin Luther King, Jr.

I've learned that holding an empowering, faithful point of view provides positive energy and more productivity. From a Power Time Management point of view, holding positive faith is a path to more fulfillment and success.

5. Nurture (grace)

God, give us grace to accept with serenity the things that cannot be changed, courage to change the things which should be changed and the wisdom to distinguish the one from the other.
— Reinhold Niebuhr

Numerous authors suggest that grace is a gift from Higher Power. We can nurture such grace in ourselves by developing a grateful heart. By this I mean, we can accentuate the positive and even tell ourselves, "I am grateful for . . ." And then we list our blessings.

At one point, I worked in an office in downtown San Francisco. The job was tough and had no connection to my best skills or my creativity. However, every morning in the shower, I repeated my "10 Blessings" to myself and lifted my own spirits. In fact, as one of the blessings, I said aloud: "I'm grateful for the prosperity provided by this job." This kept my thoughts and feelings in a graceful state of being.

Grace has been defined as the outward expression of the inward harmony of the soul. — William Hazlitt

From a Soulful Time Management perspective, ask yourself: "How can I make space so that I experience the grace I have been given?"

6. Express (art)

Let us never, never forget that we are the masters of our destiny. No one in all the universes writes our script. We do that, in co-creation with our brothers. As we rewrite our script, our brother must do likewise or leave the stage of our drama.
— Peter Erbe

As a college instructor of Comparative Religion for over 12 years, I realize that numerous individuals believe that God is creating a path for each of us. So the above Peter Erbe quote may not connect with some readers.

And still many authors and others report their belief that each person co-creates with God their life.

It's true that one can express kindness and often others will follow one's lead and return positive energy.

For example, if one nods and smiles at others, a significant number of the other people will return the gracious gesture.

Be sure to express positive things. Kind words. And even some form of creativity. Some of us may never write a book or a song, but it does take creativity to juggle our responsibilities and help our loved ones feel supported. We might even call that "expressing the art of a good, loving life."

* * *

As I mentioned earlier: **Soulful Time Management is about staying in the moment and doing that which enriches and enlivens your soul.**

Remember the Divine Gifts of love, humility, forgiveness, faith, grace and art. Do what you can to nurture and expand these elements of your life. You'll enjoy how your energy increases and your productivity improves.

Principle

You already have Divine Gifts, and you can devote efforts each week to nurture them.

Power Questions

How can you devote yourself to expressing love, humility, forgiveness, faith, grace and art? What can you do on a weekly basis?

* * *

A number of authors have observed that laughter is good for the soul. Along that line, I'll now share two articles from Steve Rizzo.

What It Means To Be Positive
by Steve Rizzo

The word "positive" seems to frustrate a lot of people. I hear people say, "How do you expect me to be positive when nothing in my life is working?" Or, "It's easy for you to be positive and feel blessed. You didn't lose someone you love or you didn't lose your job."

Maybe we should consider a more realistic interpretation of what it means to be positive. Being positive isn't always a Disney movie. I have learned that being positive isn't always about feeling good. Oddly, it's healthy to feel bad sometimes. It means you're not a robot. And being positive doesn't mean we never make mistakes.

True positivism knows that we learn from our mistakes and allows us to move forward with optimism that we are better people for having made them, richer, deeper and more resilient than before. Being positive doesn't mean that we are always smiling and enjoying every moment of our lives. Give me a break! It's realizing that sometimes it's okay to cry, mourn, and feel sad. It's not about being in control of your emotions. Hey, it's okay to sometimes get angry and lose your temper. Don't worry; your positivity license won't be revoked.

People who are generally positive have problems just like everyone else. What separates the chronically positive from everyone else is that they know that their problems won't last forever and are simply part of the process of life. Positive people are the ultimate shift-heads. That is to say, they find a way to shift their perspective and hold on to the things that bring them joy. This is a quality that keeps them from feeling victimized. Pain is unavoidable, but to a person with a positive attitude, that's all it is: pain that is not uncompounded by doubt and comparisons to past experience.

Positive people instinctively know that adversity is necessary in order to grow. We are here on Earth to experience, learn, grow and become the person we are meant to be. I can't stress enough that the filter through which we view our experiences, ultimately determines who we become.

How we choose to experience what happens to us, be it good or bad, will determine what we learn. What we learn determines how we grow, and this continued growth is what shapes who and what we become. If we can comprehend this, it will help free us from feeling victimized when times are tough, and just maybe help us to compare a challenging situation to a pop quiz in Life:101, rather than, say, the apocalypse.

(And now, Steve's second article.)

Humor Being to the Rescue—
The Importance of Humor in Business and in Life
by Steve Rizzo

The first time I can recall my sense of humor having a dramatic effect on my life was when I was in the third grade. I was performing in the play "Alice in Wonderland." No, I wasn't Alice. I was Humpty Dumpty. You know, the egghead who was damaged irreparably when he found out he didn't have Worker's Compensation. It was opening night and the auditorium was packed with parents, teachers, students and their families. I could see the rows of expectant faces, peering out from the wings of the stage. That's a lot of pressure for a third grader. The time for my scene came in the blink of an eye. There I was, sitting on the wall in my egg costume. Everything was going fine until my line, "I'm one who has spoken to a king, I am!" Well, I guess I said it with just a little too much enthusiasm because I lost my balance and fell over the back side of the wall. All the audience could hear was a giant thud! I didn't get hurt. (Not physically, anyway.) But I remember how humiliated I felt waiting behind that wall for the house to realize that falling wasn't a part of the act just yet. All I could think of was that I messed up big time. I was going to be the laughing stock of the entire school. I thought the rest of the cast would berate me for ruining the play. "And how," I wondered, "could I ever face my parents?" I wanted to run off the stage and hide, but I was frozen by fear, crouching behind the wall, an egg with egg on his face.

While the negative thoughts were running rampant in my mind, the teacher in charge was running up the steps from the first row and calling out "Steven, are you OK?" It was instinct to rely on the ability that had gotten me out of bad situations before: humor. Without missing a beat I yelled out as loud as I could, "Yeah! But I think I cracked my shell. I hope Alice doesn't mind scrambled eggs!" To my young surprise, the entire audience exploded with laughter. Hearing the laughter, I slowly stuck my head above the wall to check out what was going on. As soon as they saw my big egg head, the laughter turned into cheers and everyone in that auditorium, including the cast, was standing and chanting, "Hump-ty! Hump-ty!" Because scrambled eggs just aren't as good without a little ham, I jumped on top of the wall and proceeded to take many exaggerated bows. The teacher was begging me to please sit down before I fell off again, but I couldn't help myself. I was totally blown away by the reaction and attention I was getting. The cheers and the laughter grew louder as I took one final bow. Eventually I sat down and the play continued, and was a huge success. What happened that night that allowed me to shift from embarrassing failure to incredible success? My Humor Being came to the rescue.

In a matter of seconds there was a major shift in perspective. Just by blurting out the first obvious joke that came to my mind, I went from a klutz to a hero. An emotional transformation took place. The situation went from the most humiliating experience in my young life, to becoming the star of the show. And I'm not exaggerating when I say "star." When the play was over, I was actually signing autographs. Now that's what I call, getting my shift together!

Every time I look back on this significant incident in my life I am reminded of how important it is to be in control of my emotions in business and in life and how laughter can help me take that control. Why? Because in addition to signaling to yourself that your problem is laughable, you've also stopped the rampage of negative thinking. You've calmed your nervous system down to the point where you can shift your thoughts and think clearly, reassess the situation, bounce back and take control. That night as Humpty Dumpty, when I joined in with the laughter of the audience, I felt instant relief. I regained my confidence, took control and bounced right back up onto that wall.

Steve Rizzo is the Attitude Adjuster. You can't attend one of his keynote speeches, seminars, or read his books and leave with the same attitude. He's a personal development expert, comedian, motivational speaker, and author. His popular PBS special brought him into millions of homes. It's no surprise that he's been inducted into the Speakers Hall of Fame, an honor bestowed upon on fewer than 200 speakers worldwide since 1977.

Perhaps one of Steve's greatest achievements was the stellar degree of success he achieved as a comedian, being chosen as a SHOWTIME COMEDY ALLSTAR and sharing the stage with Jerry Seinfeld, Rodney Dangerfield, Eddie Murphy, Ellen DeGeneres and many more giants of comedy.

Of course the surprises don't stop there. What was next for this funny guy in the prime of his career? For Steve, it was to trade the standing ovations as a stand-up comedian for maximum fulfillment, and well more standing ovations as a hall of fame speaker.

Don't let the laughter fool you!

What Steve brings to the table is his captivating ability to engage the attendees with laughter as he challenges them to SHIFT their focus and way of thinking to discover greater enthusiasm, increased productivity and new levels of success. As one of his clients once said, "Never has my group learned so much and laughed so hard in one sitting! Thanks for the ride!"

Don't settle for anything less than Steve Rizzo's approach.

Because anything less… is just that.

Studies have shown that if people are having fun while they're learning they will simply absorb more information. Do you know what that adds up to? Return on Investment!

Steve Rizzo: Making a difference one group at a time!

www.steverizzo.com

www.getyourshifttogetherbook.com

* * * * * *

DISCOVER HIDDEN SECRETS OF YOUR RELATIONSHIPS AND CREATE CLOSENESS

(#5 of Increase Happiness and Enhance Relationships)

Lots of wasted time and a big loss of productivity arise because people are not willing to face the reality of expectations and hopes that someone else has. Consequently, we need to create opportunities for discussing our relationships (business, friendship, romantic, or otherwise).

Sometimes, we avoid asking if there is a possible problem because we do NOT want to put bad ideas into the other person's thoughts. Yes, there's some validity to this concern. If you ask someone "What's wrong?" their brain automatically goes and looks for something that is wrong.

However, there are often things that are creating concern for the person, but he or she has just not told you about them. *If you don't hear about these problems, you cannot improve the situation.* If some real thing cannot be adjusted, you can at least hear the person out.

Let's look at an example of how to create these opportunities.

Since I hire interns who may not be used to telling a supervisor their experience, I have a series of questions that I use:

Questions for the Intern:
1) What do you *want* with this internship?
2) What's working for you?
3) Is there something you'd like but you're not getting?
4) What ideas do you have so that we can make the internship experience better for you?
5) Again, what's working for you now? What are you grateful for that's related to this internship?

You'll notice that the final impression I leave the intern with is a positive one that's inspired by question #5: "Again, what's working for you now? What are you grateful for that's related to this internship?"

You can adapt this list of questions for a close friend (or family member):

The "How Are We Doing?" Questions
1) What do you *want* with our friendship?
2) What's working for you?
3) Is there something you'd like but you're not getting?
4) What ideas do you have so we can make our friendship experience better for you?
5) Again, what's working for you now? What are you grateful for that's related to our friendship?

It's true that for some friends this process may feel artificial. However, it can lead to handling problems that may have been festering "in the darkness."

Here are important details:
- During and immediately following your friend's description of something bad, do NOT defend yourself. Keep listening. Say something like: "I'm really concerned about that. Is there something else I need to know?"
- At the end of this conversation, you can say something like: "I really care about you and our friendship. I'm going to really think about what you said. I'm not sure how I might improve the situation. *And*, I'm glad to know how you feel."

Jack Canfield, co-author of the best-selling *Chicken Soup for the Soul* series, asks his wife: "On a scale of 1 to 10 with 10 being the best—how is our relationship going for you?" After he hears her response, he asks: "What would make it a 10?"

Jack confirms that sometimes he hears tough responses. But he says that he's glad to get this important information.

Numerous case studies show that as marriages end, one partner did not know what was deeply bothering the other person, who decided to leave the relationship.

The above process to "Face the Reality of the Relationship" can help you avoid being blindsided.

Here's a similar process to my "How Are We Doing?" Questions. Author Peter Bregman wrote about how he customized a process for one of the companies he consulted with. Managers were failing to use an employee evaluation form. Peter says he "half-designed" the revised form and then asked individual managers: *"Why won't this work for you?"* After their response, Peter replied: *"That's a good point. So how can you change it to make it work?"*

Using this process, Peter took the evaluation procedure from 50% compliance to 95% compliance by the managers. The truth is: people want their individual concerns to be heard and to be taken into account.

Research suggests that 80% of our happiness is derived from our relationships. That means it's good to keep our relationships well tuned. We keep our cars tuned up. Let's do that and better with our relationships.

Principle

Save time and heartache by finding out the reality of your relationship through the "How Are We Doing?" Questions.

Power Questions

What is your most important relationship at the moment (business, friendship, romantic, or otherwise)? How can you adapt the *"How Are We Doing?" Questions* for that relationship?

A FINAL WORD AND THE SPRINGBOARD TO YOUR DREAMS

Congratulations on your efforts with this book. Thank you for your attention. When you return to these pages again and again, you can *reenergize yourself*. You will get more value each time you review the steps covered in this book.

To gain more value and use this book as a springboard, be sure to go through it and note your new tasks *in your calendar*. Take some action. Any action towards improving skills and enlarging your life is helpful. I often say, "Better than zero."

* * *

Please consider gaining special training through my coaching (phone and in-person), workshops, presentations and Top Five Group Elite Video Training. My coaching features innovations: *Dynamic Rehearsal* and *Power Rehearsal for Crisis*. Due to my background in improvisation and training in acting, directing and screenwriting, I help clients *as I improvise dialogue* during rehearsal sessions. I coach clients to prepare for speeches and any tough or vital conversation with audiences, colleagues, sales prospects and even family members.

As you continue to work toward expanding your financial abundance and fulfillment in life, you are likely to come up against some tough situations. To be supportive I've written a number of books . . .

- Darkest Secrets of Charisma
- Darkest Secrets of Persuasion and Seduction Masters: How to Protect Yourself and Turn the Power to Good
- Darkest Secrets of Negotiation Masters
- Darkest Secrets of Making a Pitch to the Film and Television Industry
- Darkest Secrets of Film Directing
- Darkest Secrets of the Film and Television Industry Every Actor Should Know
- Darkest Secrets of Spiritual Seduction Masters
- Success Secrets of Rich, Smart and Powerful People: How You Can Use Leverage for Business Success

See my blog at
www.BeHeardandBeTrusted.com

The best to you,
Tom
Tom Marcoux,
America's Communication Coach, TFG Thought Leader, Motion Picture Director, Actor, Producer, Screenwriter
P.S. See **Free Chapters** of Tom Marcoux's 24 books at http://amzn.to/ZiCTRj   (at Amazon.com)

Titles include:
Be Heard and Be Trusted

Nothing Can Stop You This Year
Truth No One Will Tell You
10 Seconds to Wealth
Reduce Clutter, Enlarge Your Life
Wake Up Your Spirit to Prosperity — and more.
(For coaching, reach Tom Marcoux
at tomsupercoach@gmail.com)

EXCERPT FROM
DARKEST SECRETS OF PERSUASION AND SEDUCTION MASTERS: HOW TO PROTECT YOURSELF AND TURN THE POWER TO GOOD
by Tom Marcoux, America's Communication Coach
Copyright Tom Marcoux

... Now, I am in my 40's, with gray in my hair, and for 27 years I have been taking action to protect people.

And now is the time for me to protect you with the Countermeasures I reveal in this book.

Every human being needs to be able to
break the trance that a Manipulator creates.
You need to make good decisions
so you are safe and you keep growing
—and you are not cut down and crippled.

This Darkest Secrets material is so intense that I first released it only with the counterbalance of my most energizing and uplifting books, *Nothing Can Stop You This Year!* and *10 Seconds to Wealth: Master the Moment Using Your Divine Gifts.*

An interviewer asked me: "Who can be the Manipulator?"

A co-worker, a boss, a salesperson, someone you're dating, and someone you think is a friend.

Now is the time—this very minute—for me to write this book to protect you.

I must speak the truth.

These Darkest Secrets of "persuasion masters" are ...

Wait a minute! Let's say it plainly: These are the Darkest Secrets of masters of manipulation. Throughout this book, I will call these people what they are: Manipulators.

Dictionary.com defines "manipulate" as "To influence or manage shrewdly or deviously.... To tamper with or falsify for personal gain."

In this book, we will look on a manipulator as one who deviously influences someone with no concern about that person's well-being, and who causes harm to that person.

Here is the first Darkest Secret:

Darkest Secret #1:
Manipulators Make You Hurt
and Then Offer the Salve.

Manipulators would invite you to go out in the sun for hours and then sell you the salve to soothe your burns. The problem is that we don't notice that this is what they're doing.

For example, you're considering the purchase of a house. A Manipulator asks the question, "So, where would you put your TV?" This question is designed to put you into a trance.

Dictionary.com defines "trance" as "a half-conscious state, seemingly between sleeping and waking, in which ability to function voluntarily may be suspended." Let's condense this: in a trance you may not be able to function freely.

Here is the second Secret:

Darkest Secret #2:

Manipulators Put You into a Trance.

To protect yourself, you must learn to use Countermeasures to Break the Trance.

All the Countermeasures (actions you can take to break the trance) in this book will make you stronger and more capable of protecting yourself.

Now, we'll view the third Secret:

Darkest Secret #3:
Manipulators Care Nothing for You and Human Decency: They'll lie, cheat, and do whatever they need to do so they win — but their charm masks all this.

Let's return to the example of a Manipulator selling you a house. A Manipulator does not pause for an instant to see if you can truly afford the new house. The Manipulator would neglect to mention that you will not only have your mortgage payment of $900. There will be additional costs: home repairs, property tax, water, electricity, homeowner's insurance, and more. The Manipulator only emphasizes what he or she knows you want to hear: "Look! $900 is better than the $1500 you're paying for rent, which is just going down the toilet. And the $900 is an investment."

Let's go back to **Darkest Secret #1:**
Manipulators make you hurt and then offer the salve.

The Manipulator has you feeling good about the solution (salve) and feeling bad about your current life situation.

How? A Manipulator will make you hurt through questions such as:
• What bothers you about paying $1500 a month for rent? (The Manipulator will use a derisive tone when he says the

word rent.)
- What is not smart about paying rent on someone else's house instead of investing in your own house?
- How do you feel about your children walking in the neighborhood where you live now?

Do you see how these questions are designed to make you hurt enough so that you'll buy?

An interviewer asked me, "Tom, aren't these good arguments for purchasing a house?"

"What we're looking at is the *intention* of the influencer," I replied. "Let's look at our definition of a manipulator as one who deviously influences someone with no concern about that person's well-being, and who causes harm to that person. If the person truly cannot afford the house, he or she will be harmed by buying it. If the manipulator conceals the truth, the manipulator is doing harm. That's the important difference."

Some friends of mine are ethical and helpful real estate agents who truthfully reveal the whole situation and help the purchaser achieve her own goals.

In this book, we are talking about another type of person; that is, unethical Manipulators.

* * *

In any given moment, we need to remember the tactics Manipulators use. We will focus on the word D.A.R.K. so you can remember details easily and protect yourself from Manipulators.

D — Dangle something for nothing
A — Alert to scarcity
R — Reveal the Desperate Hot Button

K — Keep on pushing buttons

1. Dangle Something for Nothing

What do conmen and conwomen do to seize your attention? They make you think you're getting a "steal."

I recently saw a documentary in which a conman on a street in England showed a toy that looked like it was dancing. This fake product was actually dancing because of a hidden, invisible thread. The conman was dangling something for nothing. The Entranced Buyer thought he was getting something worth $20 for only $5. That was the trick. The Entranced Buyer felt that he was getting $15 extra of value for his $5. What the Buyer really got was something worth nothing. Similarly, I know someone who purchased a copy of a Disney movie from a street vendor in San Francisco. She brought the copy home and it was unwatchable—and the street vendor was never seen again.

An old phrase goes, "A conman cannot con someone who is not looking for something for nothing."

How to Protect Yourself from "Dangle Something for Nothing"

Stop! Get on your cell phone and talk through the "deal" with someone you know who thinks clearly. Go home. Think about it. Do some research on the Internet. Listen to your gut feelings. If the salesman or conman is too insistent, get away from that Manipulator. Get quiet. Have a cup of water. Cool down. Break the Trance!

Break the Trance and Identify the Crucial Detail

Earlier, I mentioned that a Manipulator puts you into a trance. An added problem is that we put ourselves into a trance. For example, as you read this, are you thinking about your right toe? Most likely not (unless you stubbed your toe recently). The point is that we only focus on a tiny percentage of what is going on in our life.

Around fifteen years ago, I caused myself trouble because I put myself into a trance. I discovered that under certain conditions, friendship can make you nearly deaf. Here's how: I was producing a song for a motion picture. A good friend was singing backup in the chorus. Because of our friendship, I wanted him to sound great. I completely missed the Crucial Detail. In this kind of situation, the Crucial Detail is that what truly counts is how the lead singer sounds! I made a song that I could not release. What a waste of time and money! I had put myself into a trance.

In any situation in which the Manipulator is "dangling something for nothing," we often fall into a trance and miss the Crucial Detail. The most important detail is *not* that we're saving money if we order before midnight tonight. What counts is whether the product creates a lasting, crucial benefit in our lives. And is the benefit of the product worth the cost? Some people even program themselves to make mistakes by saying, "I can't pass up a bargain." The bargain is *not* the Crucial Detail.

Secrets to Break the Trance

This is the process of B.R.E.A.K.S. It will help you remember the proven methods to break a trance.

B — Breathe
R — Relax
E — Envision
A — Act on aromas

K — Keep moving
S — Smile

Secret #1: Breathe

Remember Secret #1: Manipulators make you hurt and then offer the salve. The Manipulator wants to put you into a state of being that fills you with a sense of urgency and anxiety. Oh, no! I'm going to miss the sale!

Stop this highly vulnerable state. Take a deep breath. Do it now. Take a deep breath and let your belly "get fat" by filling it with air. As you breathe out, let your belly deflate. Breathe in through your nose and breathe out through your mouth. This is called belly-breathing. Repeat the actions of belly-breathing three times. Good. Now, do you feel different? Remember, when you are relaxed, you are strong.

End of Excerpt from
DARKEST SECRETS OF PERSUASION AND SEDUCTION MASTERS: HOW TO PROTECT YOURSELF AND TURN THE POWER TO GOOD
Copyright Tom Marcoux Media, LLC

Purchase your copy of this book (paperback or ebook) at Amazon.com or BarnesandNoble.com
See **Free Chapters** of Tom Marcoux's 24 books at http://amzn.to/ZiCTRj

ABOUT THE AUTHOR

Tom Marcoux helps people like you fulfill big dreams. Known as America's Communication Coach and TFG Thought Leader, Tom has authored 24 books with sales in 15 countries. One of his *Darkest Secrets* books rose to #1 on Amazon.com Hot New Releases in Business Life (and in Business Communication). He guides clients and audiences (IBM, Sun Microsystems, etc.) to success in job interviewing, public speaking, media relations, and branding. A member of the National Speakers Association, he is a professional coach and guest expert on TV, radio, and print, and was dubbed "the Personal Branding Instructor" by the *San Francisco Examiner*.

Tom addressed National Association of Broadcasters' Conference six years running. With a degree in psychology, Tom is a guest lecturer at **Stanford University**, DeAnza, & California State University, and teaches public speaking, science fiction cinema/literature and comparative religion at Academy of Art University. Winner of a special award at the **Emmys**, Tom wrote, directed, and produced a feature film that the distributor took to the **Cannes film market**, and the film gained international distribution. He is engaged in book/film projects *Crystal Pegasus* (children's) and *TimePulse* (science fiction). See TomSuperCoach.com and Tom's well-received blog
at www.BeHeardandBeTrusted.com

Tom Marcoux can help you with **speech writing** and **coaching for your best performance.**
As Tom says, *Make Your Speech a Pleasant Beach.*
Join Tom's Linkedin.com group: *Executive Public Speaking and Communication Power.*

At Google+: join the community "Create Your Best Life – Charisma & Confidence"

Get a **Free** report: "9 Deadly Mistakes to Avoid for Your Next Speech and 9 Surefire Methods" at http://tomsupercoach.com/freereport9Mistakes4Speech.html

Tom Marcoux has trained CEOs, small business owners, and graduate students to speak with impact and gain audiences' tremendous approval and cooperation. *Learn how to present and get thunderous applause!*

"Tom, Thanks for your coaching and work with me on revising my speech at a major university. Working with you has been so enlightening for me. Through your gentle prodding and guidance I was able to write a speech that connects with the audience. I wish everyone could experience the transformation I have undergone. You have helped me discover the warm and compelling stories that now make my speech reach hearts and uplift minds. This was truly an empowering experience. I cannot thank you enough for your great assistance." — J.S.

"Tom Marcoux has been an NAB Conference favorite [speaker] for six years. And he is very energetic."
– John Marino,
Vice President, National Association of Broadcasters, Washington, D.C.

"Using just one of Tom Marcoux's methods, I got more done in 2 weeks than in 6 months."
– Jaclyn Freitas, M.A.

Tom's Coaching features innovations:
- Dynamic Rehearsal
- Power Rehearsal for Crisis

- The Charisma Advantage that Saves Time

Become a fan of Tom's graphic novels/feature films:
Fantasy Thriller: *Jack AngelSword*
type "JackAngelSword" at Facebook.com
Science fiction: *TimePulse*
www.facebook.com/timepulsegraphicnovel

Children's Fantasy: *Crystal Pegasus*
www.facebook.com/crystalpegasusandrose
See **Free Chapters** of Tom Marcoux's 24 books
at http://amzn.to/ZiCTRj

Special Offer Just for Readers of this Book:
Contact Tom Marcoux at tomsupercoach@gmail.com for special discounts on books, coaching, workshops and presentations. Just mention your experience with this book.

www.ingramcontent.com/pod-product-compliance
Lightning Source LLC
Chambersburg PA
CBHW060516100426
42743CB00009B/1333